ENDORSEMENTS

'I can think of no better training resource for evangelism than this – it is ideally suited for use in the local church. I highly recommend it as the most inviting, user-friendly and empowering course of its kind.'
Revd Dr Mark Stibbe, *Vicar, St Andrew's Chorleywood*

'We can be grateful to J.John, the most gifted evangelist in Britain today, for showing us how to speak naturally about Jesus Christ to our friends. An extremely helpful course in an area we all find difficult.'
Revd Dr Michael Green, *Evangelist and author*

'J.John is so creative in his approach to evangelism and this course provides Christians with a measured and realistic basis for what many of us find a very difficult subject. We need all the help we can get and this course will provide us with all the help we need to become creative, courageous communicators of the Gospel.'
Fiona Castle, *author*

'Accessible, understandable, usable and practical are words I would use to describe *Breaking News*. This much needed course will help all of us to communicate our faith better. It is a great resource for any local church and should warm the heart of any leader wanting to release their people into effective witness.'
Nick Cuthbert, *writer and communicator*

'J.John's *Breaking News* will be welcomed by Christians everywhere. There is nothing we want so badly to do and feel we do so badly as evangelism. That is why this very approachable and encouraging course on personal evangelism will inspire and equip us to evangelise the world of our neighbourhoods, schools and workplaces.'
Dr Lon Allison, *Director, Billy Graham Center, Wheaton College*

'*Breaking News* is user-friendly, informative, focused and practical – an effective tool for moving the Christian from the pew to the public arena with their personal story of faith. A great resource for local churches.'
Paul C. Weaver, *General Superintendent, Assemblies of God UK*

'J.John has provided a valuable resource for the equipping of Christians to be more effective witnesses and communicators of the Good News. It needs no additional commendation, as J.John himself embodies the insights and practical approaches he shares in these six sessions.'
Dr Eddie Gibbs, *Professor of Church Growth, Fuller Seminary*

'Combine J.John's passion for "lost people", the power of the Gospel and his commitment to training and equipping, and you come up with *Breaking News*. An inspirational, intentional, concise and compelling course suitable for everyone serious about sharing their faith.'
David Shearman, *Senior Pastor, The Christian Centre, Nottingham*

'We as Christians believe that Jesus gives us abundant life – the life we all long for – and if we really know and believe that, then we will want to share that abundant life with others. And this is what J.John equips us to do, in *Breaking News*.'
Revd Carol Anderson, *Rector, All Saints Church, Beverly Hills*

'This is an exciting addition to any church and Christian who wants to fulfil the Great Commission. I believe that J.John is a true evangelist, who is recognised worldwide for his zeal and vision to spread the gospel to all nations. It's a course to challenge and encourage Christians to be doers of the Word and to take salvation to the nations.'
Pastor Ray McCauley, *Rhema, South Africa*

'Don't even think about not doing J.John's *Breaking News* course. I had the privilege of introducing J.John to Jesus Christ and since then he has continued to share that Good News with others. *Breaking News* will inspire and equip you to share the Good News of Jesus, naturally. J.John's teaching will bring you joy and that's your strength to help you shine.'
Revd Andy Economides, *Director, Soteria Trust*

'Don't you enjoy those moments when you can sit and have a discussion about something that really matters? *Breaking News* by J.John is just that. The lessons unfold like chatting with a friend – and as only a good friend can do, provides an enthusiastic push to help us get over hesitation of speaking to others about Jesus. With next day applicability J.John provides a resource that small groups, churches, seminary students and pastoral leaders should study. Quick, get some people together and experience *Breaking News*.'
Dr Carson Pue, *President, Arrow Leadership International Ministries*

'*Breaking News* is a dynamic tool to place into the hands and hearts of those who are hungry to share, in a relevant way, what they have received and to help give life to a drowning world. J.John teaches in a very relational, personal and conversational manner. He incarnates language and teaches in a story-telling fashion that gives us freedom to discover and to tell our own stories. J.John's words spring from the page to be devoured like all good stories. They demand that the reader keep on feeding upon them like water quenching a parched and thirsty land. In fact J.John is like a city planner who recognizes the necessity for the park.'
Nigel Goodwin, *Director, Genesis Arts Trust*

'Intentional evangelism is a huge aspiration for most churches, indeed most individuals. But the reality is far from the aspiration. Why? *Breaking News* analyses the hurdles we face, helps us bring them down, and gets gospel action and gospel words flowing in the right direction. Doing *Breaking News* together means that it is fun as well as educational; corporate rather than individual. I pray *Breaking News* every success in every church. This is vital if we are to be shaped by mission.'
Gerald Coates, *Team Leader, Pioneer, speaker, author, broadcaster*

'I have been encouraged, challenged and enlightened through J.John's teaching. His writings have been a great source of inspiration to me in my own ministry and I'm sure that you will find *Breaking News* to be a great blessing and a valuable resource to help you in sharing the good news with others.'
Bayless Conley, *Senior Pastor, Cottonwood Christian Center*

'J.John inspires and instructs in a most creative way. *Breaking News* shows how Christians need not fear sharing their faith. Instead, we can naturally and meaningfully share what Jesus means to us in the course of our lives. J.John combines biblical depth with hands-on practicality in inspiring us to share our faith naturally.'
Peter Chao, *Director, Eagles Communications, Singapore*

'Are you passionately in love with Jesus? The natural outpouring of that love is sharing the Good News by word and deed. In *Breaking News*, J.John challenges the mindsets that stifle presenting the Gospel. The teaching and applications he provides will help you boldly communicate the Good News with joy and ease!'
Joyce Meyer, *author and Bible teacher*

'J.John is one of our most persuasive, effective and brilliant evangelists and, thank God, he seems determined not to let all of his secrets die with him. Our churches really need this stuff! This manual will help many thousands of camouflaged Christians to overcome their fears, come out of hiding and boldly share their faith. It is clear, full of insight, packed with interest and contains all the planks we need to build the bridges of effective mission among our friends. This material is so good that leaders will be tempted to steal it and pass it off as their own. I know I was!'
Greg Haslam, *Minister, Westminster Chapel, London*

'"Beware of Greeks bearing gifts" the old adage goes. Not this time. J.John may be a Greek but this warm, purposeful training resource is one very helpful gift you don't need to beware of.'
Mark Greene, *Director, London Institute of Contemporary Christianity*

'J.John is truly a contagious Christian! Let him teach you how you can share your faith confidently and courageously.'
Lee Strobel, *author The Case for Christ*

BREAKING NEWS

A Practical Course Designed to Help You
Share God's Good News Today

J. JOHN

Authentic

16 15 14 13 12 11 10   12 11 10 9 8 7 6
Reprinted 2006, 2007, 2008 (twice)

Reprinted 2010 by Authentic Media Limited
Presley Way, Crownhill, Milton Keynes, MK8 0ES
www.authenticmedia.co.uk

Authentic Media is a division of Send The Light Ltd., a company limited by
guarantee (registered charity no. 270162)

British Library Cataloguing in Publication Data
A catalogue record for this book is available from the British Library

ISBN 978-1-86024-549-7

Cover design by fourninezero design.
Printed in Great Britain by Bell & Bain Ltd.

CONTENTS

Foreword

J.John is one of the Church's greatest communicators, blessed with gifts of teaching, humour, story-telling and integrity. *Breaking News* is practical and packed full of stories, insights and activities to stimulate the church into evangelistic action.

Evangelism is all about good news: good news for the poor, freedom for prisoners, sight for the blind, release for the oppressed, all of which proclaim the sovereign reign of God in the world today. For too long the Church has 'given up the turf' and withdrawn to the safety of church life, failing to proclaim this good news with confidence and conviction. As a consequence, our society is like a building shored-up with scaffolding but lacking firm foundations.

The current task of the Church is to reconnect imaginatively with the people of the twenty-first century. To do this, individual Christians need to communicate with confidence their own story of faith and understand how God's story still has the power to transform the lives of others in a similar way.

Taking seriously Jesus' command to go and make disciples of all nations, by word and deed, *Breaking News* provides accessible and well thought out material to assist the Church meet that challenge.

J.John knows that terrain well. He is a practitioner and writes with many years of personal experience behind him. As someone responsible to encourage the Church to think beyond its walls and to equip herself for the task of witness, I warmly commend *Breaking News* and its author to you with confidence and the expectation that God will increase the gifts of faith and love in you as you play your part in sharing the Good News and thereby hasten the coming of God's Kingdom of justice, peace and joy in the Holy Spirit. And remember: our Lord promised to be with us till the end of the time and he gave us his authority and power.

The Most Revd Dr John Sentamu
Archbishop of York

SESSION 1

THE 'WHY' OF EVANGELISM

PART 1: THE GREAT OMISSION?

At the end of Jesus' life on earth, he gave this charge to his followers:

> 'All authority in heaven and on earth has been given to me.
> Therefore go and make disciples of all nations, baptising them
> in the name of the Father and of the Son and of the Holy
> Spirit.' Matthew 28:18–19

Unfortunately, many of us are like Arctic rivers: frozen at the mouth. Most of us have missed opportunities to talk about Jesus with our relatives, friends, neighbours and work colleagues because we've 'frozen' on the spot.

But why do we freeze?

Try this:

Break into pairs and ask yourselves: If I had to share the Good News of Jesus with my friends:

• What would hold me back?

....
....

• How might I approach the task creatively?

....
....

- If I weren't a Christian, how would I react if I were engaged in a discussion about my beliefs?

  . . . .

  . . . .

- What would make me comfortable/uncomfortable in the way that I was approached?

  . . . .

  . . . .

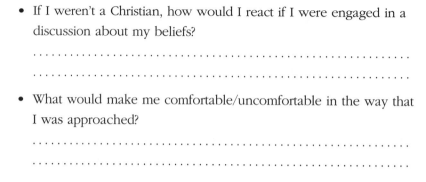

We shouldn't be worried about what we do *not* know, but share what we *do* know. Jesus taught profound truths in very simple ways.

Clearly, many of us have reservations and fears when it comes to evangelising. The Bible says, 'Fearing people is a dangerous trap' (Proverbs 29:25, NLT) – and this, for me, sums up our biggest fear: other people. Fear comes in many forms, but here are four common ones:

A. Fear of Being Inadequate

We shouldn't be worried about what we do *not* know, but share what we *do* know. Jesus taught profound truths in very simple ways. He said, 'Unless you change and become like little children, you will never enter the kingdom of heaven' (Matthew 18:3). So it's important for us not to panic but to be confident about the Good News that we have to offer.

B. Fear of Losing Reputation

We are often paralysed by what others will say or think of us. Yet the Bible says that Jesus 'made himself nothing' for us (Philippians 2:7). That's our example to follow. At Golgotha when Jesus was crucified, he had no reputation to lose. So why should we worry about ours?

However, that doesn't mean to say that we shouldn't present the message graciously, sensitively and with care.

C. Fear of Rejection

None of us likes to be rejected. It is hard to handle, since we have a built-in need for love and acceptance.

D. Fear of Appearing Hypocritical

Do our lives demonstrate the difference that the Gospel makes? Or are we living so inconsistently, having succumbed to the attitudes and moral standards around us, that we are no longer credible?

Jesus made it clear that if we are going to follow him, we should not be surprised that some people will reject us. After all, he – of all people – was 'despised and rejected' (Isaiah 53:3). The Bible says that 'even in his own land and among his own people he was not accepted' (John 1:11, NLT).

The Greek word for witness is *'marturia'* – from which we derive the word 'martyr'. As the apostle Paul made clear to Timothy, 'everyone who wants to live a godly life in Christ Jesus will be persecuted' (2 Timothy 3:12).

Many did accept Jesus but many also rejected him. So we shouldn't be surprised sometimes that rejection is part of the process of sharing the Good News of Jesus.

We are not told to provoke it or invite it but we are told to expect it.

Talking point:

When you've tried to share the Good News of Jesus, how have people reacted?

- What works, and what doesn't?
  . . . .
  . . . .

• What lessons have you learned from your previous attempts?

....

....

PART 2: WHAT IS EVANGELISM?

Sometimes, good words can end up feeling like bad words within our culture. The verb 'to evangelise' – which is clearly biblical, being used 52 times in the New Testament – is looked upon with suspicion today by many people who don't want religion shoved down their throats.

Try this:

Spend a few moments, individually, writing down one or two definitions of 'evangelism'.

• What does it mean?

....

....

• How would you define it in no more than 25 words, using no theological language or religious jargon?

....

....

So what does 'evangelism' mean?

Evangelism is the practice of sharing the Gospel of Jesus Christ.

The word 'Gospel' means good news. The 'Gospel' to the first-century followers of Christ was indeed NEWS – BREAKING NEWS – of 'victory over the enemy' made possible through Jesus Christ.

Evangelism is to pass on GOOD NEWS or as my friend, Greg Downes says, 'Evangelism means to hand out invitations to a free party that is "out of this world".'

William Temple, Archbishop of Canterbury during the Second World War, penned the following definition:

> To evangelise is to present Jesus Christ in the power of the Holy Spirit, that people may come to put their trust in God through him, to accept him as their Saviour and serve him as their King in the fellowship of the Church.
>
> William Temple
> *Towards the Conversion of England*

'Evangelism means to hand out invitations to a free party that is "out of this world".'

Let's remember at this point that words mean nothing without actions. In Luke 4:18–19, we find Jesus in the synagogue reading from Isaiah 61:

> *'The Spirit of the Lord is on me, because he has anointed me to preach good news to the poor. He has sent me to proclaim freedom for the prisoners and recovery of sight for the blind, to release the oppressed, to proclaim the year of the Lord's favour.'*

It's clear from this, and the life of Jesus, that the *proclamation* of the Good News (**words**) is one side of the coin, the other being a *demonstration* of the Good News (**works**). We can't just throw words at people, however good the words are.

Just as faith without works is dead, so, too, evangelism without godly action is hypocrisy.

Talking point:

- Do we endeavour to 'practise what we preach'?
  . . . .
  . . . .

- And do we believe what we're hoping to share with others?

  ....

  ....

- How can we ensure that our conversations have integrity and authenticity?

  ....

  ....

PART 3: WHY SHOULD WE EVANGELISE?

1. The Command of Christ

Jesus gave us clear instructions to spread the Good News. He has commanded us to 'go and make disciples'. This has become known as the 'Great Commission' (which can be found in Matthew 28:19–20):

> 'Therefore go and make disciples of all nations, baptising them
> in the name of the Father and of the Son and of the Holy Spirit,
> and teaching them to obey everything I have commanded you.
> And surely I am with you always, to the very end of the age.'

In this passage, we are told to do three things: to **make** disciples (people need to become committed to Jesus Christ), to **mark** disciples (baptising them), and to **mature** disciples (helping them to grow in wisdom and faith).

Evangelisation is not just about bringing people to a point of decision, but is also about helping them to embark on a lifetime of obedience to Jesus.

A church that does not do its best to help others to become Christians is disobedient and guilty of the sin of omission. Jesus said, 'All those who love me will do what I say' (John 14:23, NLT).

The Church is about three things:

1. *Looking up* – worship

Worship is celebrating the presence of God over his creation and among his people. It includes our response in adoration, confession and a desire to encounter his power, truth and beauty. True worship is inwardly transforming and outwardly focusing, as we share God's compassion for a world in desperate need of him.

2. *Looking in* – well-being

Well-being is the closest we can get in English to translating the Hebrew word 'shalom' – peace. It signifies a balanced life that is blessed by God. It cannot be experienced in isolation but flows from relationships that are accepting, affirming, accountable and transforming. They provide the context in which we can grow into our God-given potential and make our contribution to the ministry of the whole church, both with the believing community and to the surrounding needy community and world.

3. *Looking out* – witness

Witness is our first-hand testimony in both words and actions to what God has done FOR us in Christ through the sacrifice of his Son on the Cross, to what Christ through his Spirit continues to do IN us to make us more like himself, as well as to what he achieves THROUGH us to continue his ministry in the world.

Sadly, the Church over the years has had an imbalance, often neglecting witness and focusing more on worship and well-being. Do you and your church have a healthy balance of worship, well-being and witness (at least 33 per cent for each)?

Assessment:

What percentages would you assign to the three categories in the case of your church?

Worship   . . . . per cent

Well-being   . . . . per cent

Witness   . . . . per cent

Total   100 per cent

2. The Compassion of Christ

If we really love God, we will love other people. Jesus was deeply moved by human needs. In Matthew 9:36–38 we read:

> *When he saw the crowds, he had compassion on them, because they were harassed and helpless, like sheep without a shepherd. Then he said to his disciples, 'The harvest is plentiful but the workers are few. Ask the Lord of the harvest, therefore, to send out workers into his harvest field.'*

In the original Greek, 'compassion' is a very strong word, full of deep, gut-level feeling and emotion. It's about being moved to the depths of one's heart, 'suffering with someone' by entering into their despair and pain.

Evangelism is not just about numbers; we count people because people count. Because we are made in the image of God, every individual is a person of intrinsic worth.

Evangelism is not just about numbers; we count people because people count. Because we are made in the image of God, every individual is a person of intrinsic worth.

Try this:

Spend a few minutes in prayer. You may need to ask God to forgive you for not always being compassionate in your life. Pray for a deeper understanding of the needs of the people you have met during the day, or over the past week, or someone whom God especially brings to mind as you prayerfully ponder this point. And in the quiet, ask God to use you to help them. Then prayerfully consider this question:

'I will build my
church.'
Jesus Christ

- Is there one thing you can do to live simply, so that others can simply live?

....

....

Pray that God will give you discernment and compassion to become more aware of the needs of people when you come into contact with them.

3. The Conviction of Christ

The Church is a living organism, and all living things grow. Jesus was committed to the growth of his Church. 'Jesus went through all the towns and villages, teaching in their synagogues, preaching the good news of the kingdom and healing every disease and sickness' (Matthew 9:35). So not only did Jesus use words and works but also wonders.

Jesus also said, 'I will build my church' (Matthew 16:18). It's his Church and he wants it to grow. Many of his parables use growth terminology and imagery.

What's more, the New Testament demonstrates numerical growth. At the start of the book of Acts, we read that the number of disciples was around 120. Towards the end of the book, as the disciples had spread the Word, they numbered 'many thousands' (Acts 21:20). That's serious growth! But the growth Jesus has in mind results not just in bigger crowds of believers, but also in people being transformed by the Gospel of the kingdom, so that they make a difference in their communities and in society at large.

4. The Consummation of Christ's Kingdom

Jesus said, 'This gospel of the kingdom will be preached in the whole world as a testimony to all nations, and then the end will come' (Matthew 24:14).

So, one of the prerequisites of Christ's return is the spread of the Christian message to the whole world. The Bible does not say that there will be world conversion before Christ returns, but it does say there will be world *evangelisation*. Everyone must hear, although not everyone will respond.

As the world's population increases, the task gets harder. At the time of the Great Commission, the world population was about 170 million. Today it is around 6.7 billion. There are now 218 nations and 271 major languages.

Many of us have heard opportunity knocking at our door but, as someone once said, by the time we unhooked the chain, pushed back the bolt, turned two locks and switched off the burglar alarm, it was gone. We are all faced with great opportunities brilliantly disguised as impossible situations. Our response is so often too little, too late, or the knock on the door is simply ignored or goes unheeded because we are too preoccupied with our own agendas.

> Many of us have heard opportunity knocking at our door, but by the time we unhooked the chain, pushed back the bolt, turned two locks and switched off the burglar alarm, it was gone.

Talking point:

First, read this true story, and then discuss the questions that follow.

> A Christian family was on holiday, travelling down a road, when they saw a suitcase fly off the top of a car going in the opposite direction. They stopped to pick it up, but the driver of the other car hadn't noticed and so didn't stop. The only clue to the driver's identity was a gold coin with the inscription 'Given to Otis Sampson on his retirement by Portland Cement Company.'
>
> After extensive correspondence, Otis Sampson was located and contacted. He wrote a letter telling them to discard the suitcase and contents and send only the gold coin. Mr Sampson used the phrase 'my most precious possession' several times to describe the coin. They sent it to him with a letter about their own most precious possession – Jesus Christ. A year later, they received a Christmas package. In it was the gold coin. Mr Sampson wrote, 'You will be happy to know we have become Christians and active members of a church. We want you to have this gold coin. I am 74 and my wife is 72. You were the first people to tell us about Jesus. Now he is our most precious possession.'

- How many of your relatives, friends, neighbours or work colleagues know about the treasure you possess?

  . . . .
  . . . .

- How infectious is your love of Jesus?

  . . . .
  . . . .

- If you have forgotten that Jesus is your most precious treasure, how can you help to remind yourself of the wonderful gift you have received?

  . . . .

  . . . .

PART 4: SEEING THE BIG PICTURE

It's even harder to evangelise others when we ourselves don't fully grasp the Good News we're called to share. So it's crucial, if we are to be effective communicators, to remind ourselves continually of the Good News itself – and to establish, in our mind's eye, the 'bigger picture' of our faith and where we fit into it.

Try this:

Taking a blank piece of paper cut it into six jigsaw pieces. Jumble up the pieces and then try, as a group, to put them back together.

Now, do the same thing – but with a full-page *image* taken from a magazine.

Ask yourselves, 'Why is it so much easier to do the jigsaw with a picture on it?' In the same way, if we can see and understand the Big Picture of God's story, then we can put the whole story together and explain it to people more confidently.

To communicate the optimism and hope of the Gospel, we need to be able to explain the Big Picture of God's positive attitude and dealings with humanity throughout history. The whole sweep of God's story is presented to us in the Old and New Testaments, and there is no substitute for reading through the whole Bible from start to finish to understand this better. Just reading the Bible for 15 minutes a day will enable you to read through the Bible in a year.

In Ephesians, Paul provides us with a helpful snapshot summary of that history. To end this session, read it together.

Read Ephesians 1:3—2:13

How we praise God, the Father of our Lord . . .

We can break this passage into seven sections (see the Appendix for Bible references):

1. Creation (the relationship between God and humanity)
2. Chaos (sin and separation)
3. Covenant (covenant blessing and promise)
4. Christ (the Mediator)
5. Conqueror (Jesus rises from the dead)
6. Certainty (new life by the Spirit and our inheritance assured)
7. Completion (the rescue completed)

Try this:

Try to summarise the Big Picture in one or two sentences.

. . . .

. . . .

Talking point:

- Who took the initiative to mend the relationship between God and humankind?

. . . .

. . . .

- Think about those who are not (or not yet) Christians. What does the passage say about their present relationship to God and their future?

  . . . .

  . . . .

- Think about those who are believers in Christ. What does the passage say about their present relationship with God and their future?

  . . . .

  . . . .

- How does knowing and understanding the Big Picture help us in sharing our faith?

  . . . .

  . . . .

A Prayer

Father, Son and Holy Spirit, Creator, Redeemer and Comforter, thank you that you work in perfect harmony as you create and sustain our world and the universe. Forgive us when we neglect to spread the news that you are Good News. May your perfect love cast out our fear. And please help us to encourage each other, as we reflect on the wonderful treasure you have given us — forgiveness for the past, new life today and a hope for the future. We want to pass on this Good News. So please inspire us to be creative, courageous communicators of the Gospel. Amen.

SESSION 2

WHAT IS THE GOOD NEWS OF CHRISTIANITY?

PART 1: RECAPPING 'THE "WHY" OF EVANGELISM'

In the first session, we asked 'Why *don't* we evangelise?' and we considered some of our fears: of inadequacy, of losing our reputation, of appearing hypocritical and of rejection.

Then, we asked, 'Why *should* we evangelise'? – we evangelise because:

1. The C . . . . of Christ
2. The C . . . . of Christ
3. The C . . . . of Christ
4. The C . . . . of Christ's Kingdom

Finally, we looked at the 'Big Picture', to gain an overview of the story of God's involvement with our world. We read Ephesians 1:3—2:13, and saw that the passage could be broken into seven categories:

1. Creation
2. Chaos
3. Covenant
4. Christ the Mediator
5. Christ the Conqueror
6. Certainty

7. Completion

We reminded ourselves that the Gospel is not so much about a series of facts to convey, but good news to share about a person to be encountered, who will make a profound difference in our life.

Now, we'll begin to look at how we can get the message right.

Talking point:

Spend a few minutes discussing what struck you most about the first session, and how it might have equipped you to think differently about evangelism this week. Does anyone have a story to share about an experience of evangelism this last week?

PART 2: GETTING THE MESSAGE RIGHT

If we don't explain a message clearly, it can have disastrous consequences! Take the story of a couple travelling through Asia with their much-loved pet dog. When they entered one town, they found a restaurant – and with the aid of gestures and a phrase book, they persuaded the waiter to take the dog away and feed him.

Imagine how they felt, therefore, when their beloved dog was presented to them, grilled and neatly served on a plate. They had communicated a message – but it was the wrong one!

Talking point:

We've all been the victims, and the perpetrators, of miscommunication. It can happen in so many different ways. Share with each other examples of how you've tried to say one thing but have been understood in a completely different way altogether.

• What have you learned from the experience?

....

....

Sometimes we fail to get the message because we have stopped listening while the other person is speaking! We might like to reflect on how well we listen to others.

What is a Christian?

I carried out some research on the streets to ask people whether they believed they were a 'Christian'. And I received some intriguing responses.

'My great auntie used to play the organ in church,' said one, inferring that this was enough.

'Are you a Christian?' I asked another. 'I'm Church of England!' came the reply.

A third said 'Yes,' she was a Christian, 'because I got married in a church.'

Talking point:

Before we really begin to share the Good News, it's vital to ask ourselves, 'What is a Christian?'

• What helps to mark me out as different?

....

....

- How would I define what a Christian is, and how would I sum that up to someone in a few words?

....

....

God-Talk: Are They Thinking What You're Thinking?

When we talk to people about God, we might assume that we share the same understanding of the character and personality of God. Yet people outside (and sometimes even within) the Christian faith may have a very different way of thinking about God – and we should be aware of that when we start any conversation.

To think about:

- In what ways has your own understanding of God changed since you became a follower of Christ?

....

....

It's not just a case of whether a person believes in God – but what sort of God they believe in.

Try this:

This is an exercise designed to show the different ways people 'see' God. It shows, too, how different people will have different perceptions about the rest of the Christian faith. We don't have time to look in detail at how they see every aspect of the story we tell – but if we use this as an example, we can get an idea.

Ask a different member of the group in turn to read one of the following statements:

Statement 1: My idea of God is an irritable old man in heaven who needs to be handled carefully, unless you want something nasty to happen to you. His favourite phrase is 'Stop it!' He seems to delight in lightning bolts and plagues.

Statement 2: My idea of God is some sort of all-powerful being who, for reasons that no one can understand, enjoys experimenting on people to see how much pain and misery they can put up with. He seems to be fond of disease, accidents and injustice.

Statement 3: My idea of God is that he's pretty much absent most of the time from Planet Earth, or if he is around, he leaves the phone off the hook.

Statement 4: My idea of God is of someone who really hangs out with Nature – trees, flowers and fluffy little lambs. In towns, you can feel close to God if you have the right sort of music and candles and can meditate. I think she likes pastel colours.

Statement 5: My idea of God is that he's like an uncle I had as a child, whose entire purpose in life seemed to be to give me money, regardless of what I had done. He makes me feel better and is really useful when the Prozac doesn't work . . .

Statement 6: My idea of God is well . . . I dunno. Sort of vague, really. I mean, I think he is inside me. Maybe he's not a he. I'm not sure he likes anything, really. He just is. Maybe. Whatever . . .

Statement 7: My idea of God? Get real! The only God there is, comes from our minds. There is no actual God out there. If you believe in him, her or it, then he, she or it, is real to you. Me, I choose not to believe, so it doesn't exist. Not for me . . .

It's hard to define God on one level. After all, God is a mystery to be encountered and experienced, not a problem to be solved. God cannot be boxed into the narrow confines of our expectations.

However, the God of the Bible is a mystery that has been made known. We can't know everything there is to know about God, but we can know enough to know him.

'God created man in his own image and man has been returning the compliment ever since.'

The word 'mystery' in the Bible means not a puzzle we have to solve, but something we could never fathom, unless God makes it known. Look up Romans 16:25–26 and Colossians 1:26.

Many popular concepts of God are wrong because they are based on what individuals would like to believe God is like, or a notion of God that they reject, rather than what he is actually like. To paraphrase the great thinker Blaise Pascal, 'God created man in his own image and man has been returning the compliment ever since.'

Talking point:

- Have you ever stopped to think that your perception of God might be different from other people's?

  . . . .
  . . . .

- Share your own perception of God in the light of the seven statements. How do your views differ within the group?

  . . . .
  . . . .

- How might this affect the way you try to talk about God with others?

  . . . .
  . . . .

The renowned North American sociologist Robert N. Bellah conducted a survey asking people for their idea of what God was like. One woman called Sheila responded like this:

> God is so loving; he would never judge anyone. God doesn't require people to go to Church. God doesn't expect people to live moral lives.

R.N. Bellah concluded that this woman was not a Christian, but a 'Sheilaist' – as she had created a religion based purely on her own subjective opinions.

It's sometimes tempting to miss out certain aspects of God's character to make God sound more, well, marketable. It's easier, of course, to sell the idea of a 'nice' God to someone rather than, say, a God of judgement. But we're neither about the art of selling, nor of making people 'feel' good. We are instead trying to convey the true message that God himself has revealed who he is, how he relates to the world he has created and sustains, and how we can know him, overcoming the alienation caused by our willful disobedience and waywardness.

PART 3: THE GOSPEL IN A NUTSHELL

The 'Good News' that we want to share with people can be summed up in four simple statements. These don't cover every single nuance of the entire biblical sweep of history, of course. If you're sitting on a train or talking to a neighbour, you won't always have time to explain everything in the finest detail! But these summary points should help you to communicate the message in a short, succinct way, as you try to talk with others about God.

Here are the statements:

God formed us: Design

In the first book of the Bible, Genesis (Hebrew for 'beginnings'), we are told, 'God created man in his own image . . . and it was very good' (Genesis 1:27–31).

God the Creator formed us as the crown and pinnacle of his creation – in his likeness.

Sin deformed us: Disorder

God's good creation did not stay that way for long and Genesis 3 records the story of the advent of sin into the world.

Notice that God gave Adam and Eve GENERAL PERMISSION:

'You are free to eat from any tree in the garden' (2:16)

and SINGULAR PROHIBITION:

'But you must not eat from the tree of the knowledge of good and evil' (2:17).

Adam and Eve chose to rebel against God's one prohibition – (3:6) and sin contaminated the world like a virus infects a computer and brings disorder and chaos.

Sin has been defined as 'a three-letter word with "I" in the middle.'

The testimony of the Bible and experience is that each one of us has had our own Eden experience and rebelled against God's good governance and strayed from his presence. The Bible account tells us that Adam and Eve's disobedience caused them to be excluded from the garden. In other words, it resulted in their alienation. They had to suffer the consequences of their attitudes and actions. We live with those consequences today.

Christ transforms us: Deliverance

Since the earliest times, the serpent in the story has been seen as representing the devil, who led humankind in rebellion against God. At the end of the account, God promises the serpent that a descendent of Eve 'will crush your head' (Genesis 3:15).

Thousands of years later, the apostle Paul was to declare that Jesus Christ 'disarmed the powers and authorities . . . made a public spectacle of them, triumphing over them by the cross' (Colossians 2:15).

The Cross of Christ is God's great act of rescue. 'Jesus' literally means 'God saves' or a modern paraphrase would be 'God-to-the-rescue'. God has come to our rescue in Christ and delivered us from disorder and death through Christ's blood shed on the Cross. His resurrection from the dead and subsequent ascension into heaven declares his victory over sin and death.

Scripture informs us: Decision

In John's gospel we read, 'To all who RECEIVED him, to those who BELIEVED in his name, he gave the right to become children of God' (John 1:12).

Each of us has a decision to make. To decide to become a Christian is to:

BELIEVE In Jesus Christ and his message, repenting of our sins and placing our confidence in him.

RECEIVE Jesus Christ into our life by God's Holy Spirit who strengthens us to validate our faith in thought, word and deed.

FOLLOW Jesus Christ in every area of our life, for we are now part of his new creation and belong to his family.

Try this:

Try to create an outline, using basic symbols for each of the points, to help you remember these four crucial statements. Keep it very simple and memorable. Once you've created your diagram, try to take someone in your group step by step through the story by using your outline.

Share your symbols with other members of your group and see if someone has come up with a clearer 'shape' than you have. Some of us are stronger visually than verbally.

PART 4: WE BELIEVE . . .

The Church spent several hundred years debating the key elements of 'doctrine', so as to avoid false teaching and heresy. Finally, at the Council of Nicea in AD 325 (some of you may have grown up with the designation CE [Common Era] and may not recognise the Latin-rooted AD), the Early Church leaders agreed on the following description of our faith, known as the Nicene Creed. To conclude, and to remind us of what we believe, read this together. You might decide to try to learn it by the end of the course:

We believe in one God,
The Father, the Almighty,
Maker of heaven and earth,
Of all that is, seen and unseen.

We believe in one Lord, Jesus Christ,
The only Son of God,
Eternally begotten of the Father,
God from God, Light from Light,

True God from true God,

Begotten, not made,

Of one Being with the Father.

Through him, all things were made.

For us and for our salvation

He came down from heaven:

By the power of the Holy Spirit

He became incarnate from the Virgin Mary,

And was made man.

For our sake, he was crucified under Pontius Pilate;

He suffered death and was buried.

On the third day he rose again

In accordance with the Scriptures;

He ascended into heaven

And is seated at the right hand of the Father.

He will come again in glory to judge the living and the dead;

And his kingdom will have no end.

We believe in the Holy Spirit, the Lord, the giver of life,

Who proceeds from the Father and the Son.

With the Father and the Son, he is worshipped and glorified.

He has spoken through the Prophets.

We believe in one holy catholic and apostolic Church.

We acknowledge one baptism for the forgiveness of sins.

We look for the resurrection of the dead,

And the life of the world to come. Amen.

A Prayer

Creator God, thank you that you designed us and even in our rebellion reached out to deliver us from the disorder caused by our sin.

Empower us by your Spirit that we might have strength, courage and clarity of thought to communicate this transforming message compassionately and effectively. Amen.

SESSION 3

WHAT IS FRIENDSHIP EVANGELISM?

PART 1: RECAPPING 'WHAT IS THE GOOD NEWS?'

In the previous session, we asked, 'What is the Good News of Jesus?' We thought about 'getting the message right', and asked ourselves, 'What is a Christian?' We considered how important it is to understand our audience, and reminded ourselves that different people have different ways of seeing God, so we mustn't presume *they're* thinking exactly what we're thinking.

Finally, we thought about the Good News as a whole, and broke the Christian story into four parts:

1. God formed us: Design
2. Sin deformed us: Disorder
3. Christ transforms us: Deliverance
4. Scripture informs us: Decision

Try this:

Last week, we explained to others how we might communicate these basic statements of the Christian story. Spend a few minutes refreshing your memory, and then explain these four statements once more with someone. As you listen to each other, take particular note of any biblical terms or religious jargon that might need explaining or should be avoided in order to make the message as clear and accessible as possible.

PART 2: EVANGELISM BEGINS AT HOME!

'You will receive power when the Holy Spirit comes on you; and you will be my witnesses in Jerusalem, and in all Judea and Samaria, and to the ends of the earth'

The book of Acts, which tells how the Good News began to spread, records in its opening chapter the words of Jesus. He said, 'You will receive power when the Holy Spirit comes on you; and you will be my witnesses in Jerusalem, and in all Judea and Samaria, and to the ends of the earth' (Acts 1:8).

That sounds quite frightening. How can we go to the ends of the earth and spread the Gospel? Jesus told the disciples to start in Jerusalem, precisely because *that was where they were*. It was the scene of their bleakest moment, when they deserted Jesus as he was crucified. It was also the place where they felt most threatened, and where they wanted to conceal their presence. But it was also the starting point for their global mission. The Word would not spread to the ends of the earth unless it started where they were – at home – and this was their first and toughest challenge! No wonder they needed the message of assurance that they would receive the power of the Holy Spirit in Jerusalem to witness to Jesus.

So what does 'Jerusalem' mean to us? It is symbolic of our home – our immediate family, friends, neighbours and work colleagues. As it was for the disciples, it might also be the place of our greatest failings and fears. But unless we start there, our own mission – to spread the Good News – will never get off the ground.

In Acts 20:20, the Bible tells us that the Gospel – the Good News – spread 'from house to house'. It should, likewise, go from our home to the homes of others we already know.

Historical note: Furthermore, we must recognise that 'house' in the New Testament refers to the household of a pre-industrial city. Before factories and offices, nearly all business and trade was undertaken in and from the home. So the house signified much more than a domestic family; it was a basic economic unit of society. Associated with the typical 'house' would be servants, clientele (customers) and the friends of the family. About 80 per cent of the working population consisted of labourers. The Gospel spread in the early centuries from household to household, an interconnected network of relationships.

Try this:

The Bible records how people's natural impulse upon meeting Jesus or hearing the Good News was to go and share it with others. Find the following verses and fill in the blanks in the sentences below. After reading each verse, pause for a moment, and imagine that you are in the shoes of the person featured. Ask yourself, how do you think each person felt? What prompted their response? Why did they go and tell the people they told?

1. John 1:41–42: Andrew brought . . . .
2. John 1:43–45: Philip told . . . .
3. John 4:28–30: The Samaritan woman told . . . .
4. Luke 5:27–32: Levi invited his . . . .
5. Acts 16:25–34: The Philippian jailer shared with his . . . .

There are three natural groups of people within our 'Jerusalem'. It's important for us to identify them:

1. **Kin** (our family and close friends)
2. **Community** (those we meet regularly, such as work colleagues, our neighbours, school teachers)
3. **Interest** (those we share the same meeting place with, such as the golf club, gym or toddler group)

We're going to focus on 'Jerusalem' here, because that's where we have to start. But as we develop our skills at friendship evangelism, they should not be restricted to individuals we already know. A true witness must also ask regularly 'To whom can I be a friend?' Then we'll begin to have the confidence to spread the word into 'Judea' and 'Samaria' – the friends and contacts we don't see so often, followed by those who we know but don't get on with – and then to 'the ends of the earth' (those people we've never even met).

Try this:

So it's time to identify those in 'Jerusalem' who we haven't yet told about the Good News of Jesus Christ. Spend a few minutes writing down the names of those people you know well, who you haven't told about Jesus.

Write down the name of the person in the relevant 'Jerusalem' – Kin, Community or Interest. Where a person falls into more than one category, put them in the overlapping circles.

Ask the Lord to guide you to two people in each category and share their names with two other people in the group. Covenant to pray for them at least once a week. Hold each other accountable and provide encouragement in the coming days and weeks by recording the ways in which your prayers are being answered.

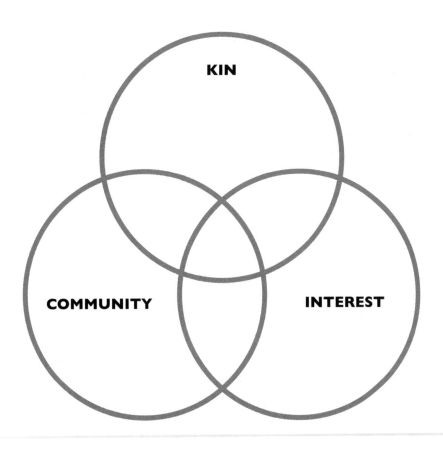

KIN   COMMUNITY   INTEREST

....
....
....
....
....
....
....
....
....

PART 3: BUBBLING OVER!

My friend Greg Downes was in a supermarket. As he passed the sugar section it occurred to him that by careful dieting he had lost the equivalent of 15 bags of sugar – 35lb. He had an idea to pick up 15 bags of sugar and walk around with them, so that the reality of the weight loss would sink in and he would be reminded never to put it on again. When he was walking round the aisles with all this sugar, an elderly woman enquired, 'What are you doing?' Greg replied, 'I've just lost all this weight.' Later he was at the frozen foods section and heard the woman gossiping to another: 'I've just met a man who has lost 15 bags of sugar in weight.' When he got to the checkout, the cashier remarked, 'Oh, you're the man who has lost 15 bags of sugar in weight!' Good news travels fast.

> The best evangelism is not driven by feelings of guilt or duty, but is a natural by-product of falling deeply in love with Jesus.

Michael Marshall states that evangelism will happen naturally when the Church is at 'apostolic bubbling point'. What he means is that the best evangelism is not driven by feelings of guilt or duty, but is a natural by-product of falling deeply in love with Jesus.

It is, quite simply, the overflow of the abundant life that Christ has made available to us. It is very difficult to get half-full Christians to overflow!

A missionary is not someone who crosses the sea; a missionary is someone who sees the Cross. When we have encountered the love of Christ, that love compels us.

Whether we go a thousand miles or a hundred yards – the most difficult part of the journey is the last three feet!

Friendship evangelism is no ordinary exercise, no mundane task which we're obliged, out of duty, to tackle. Instead, it is driven by the twin values of compassion and love.

Take Bob Geldof. When he saw on the news that millions of people in Ethiopia were starving to death, he didn't sit back and leave the problem to someone else. He did something about it and organised Band Aid and LIVE 8. He felt compassion and turned it into positive action.

Like Geldof, one of Jesus' main attributes was compassion – for the people he met. He didn't see them as statistics (do we?). Instead, he saw their needs, felt their pain, shared their joy, and wanted to see their lives transformed for good.

Jesus doesn't call you to make disciples because he wants to give you a tough or embarrassing task to earn your place in heaven. Instead, he asks you to continue his work, which was birthed, from the start, by a very practical love. If we love God and our neighbour, as the Bible calls us to, then the natural overflow of that love will be to introduce our neighbours to the God we love.

> 'We cannot stop telling about the wonderful things we have seen and heard.'

There are some things in life we just can't help talking about. If you've had a child, you'll know how hard it is not to talk about the good news of your new arrival. (And as they continue to grow, you'll find it hard not to keep boasting to your friends and relatives of their progress!) If you've ever fallen in love, you'll know how hard it is to contain your excitement: your natural reaction is to tell others how wonderful your boyfriend or girlfriend is – it's an overflow of your heart. You can't keep it in. Similarly, if your sports team wins the league, the cup, or even just a match, it's natural to share your delight with others. If you support a winning team, everyone knows – but does everyone know you're on God's side?

In Acts 4:20, when the religious leaders told Peter and John to stop talking publicly about Jesus, Peter replied, 'We cannot stop telling about the wonderful things we have seen and heard' (NLT). They couldn't help themselves!

When it comes to evangelism, YOU CAN'T GIVE AWAY WHAT YOU HAVEN'T GOT.

You and I need to walk in intimacy with God, our hearts ablaze with the love of Christ. Then we will find that evangelism happens as a by-product – an overflow of our burning hearts.

Talking point:

Spend a few minutes talking with each other.

- What things do you get excited about and can't stop talking about?

  . . . .

  . . . .

- Why do you get so excited about these things?

  . . . .

  . . . .

- Why can't you stop talking about them?

  . . . .

  . . . .

- How does this compare with when you are talking about Jesus?

  . . . .

  . . . .

- Do you see yourself as bringing good news – or do you feel more like you're about to offend someone?

  . . . .

  . . . .

To think about:

Every day we communicate some message or other. Replay in your mind some conversations you've had in the last few days. Have you been a carrier of gossip or negative thoughts, or of good news?

PART 4: TURNING THOUGHTS INTO ACTION

Have you ever stopped to wonder why people who aren't yet Christians come to church? I once read some fascinating statistics:

1 per cent come because they were visited by Christians

2 per cent come because of the church programme – they've come along to a holiday club, a senior citizens' lunch, toddler group, and so on

3 per cent come because of bereavement

3 per cent come because of Sunday school

6 per cent walk through the door because they see some publicity

8 per cent come because of some personal contact they've had with the minister or church staff

And 77 per cent come because friends or relatives invited them

It's easy enough to read statistics, but this one is worth stopping to think about for a moment: 77 per cent of people come to church because friends or relatives invite them.

Have you contributed to this statistic?

We also have to acknowledge the fact that the problem may be that my church isn't the kind of place I would want to invite any of my friends to visit. What changes would need to take place before I felt confident that my friends would be likely to have a positive experience?

Breaking Down the Barriers Between Us

Remember that you can't fish from a pond in which there are no fish. If we spend all our time with other Christians, we won't be in a position to invite people along to church in the first place. But even if we don't spend lots of leisure time with those who are not yet Christians, we'll have seen, from the list of names we wrote down in Session 2, that we come into contact with many people in our everyday lives that we can, if we have the courage, share the Good News with.

Sometimes, we think that the barriers between them and us are so great that we can't possibly talk about our faith. Yet Jesus showed us that barriers aren't always as great as they first appear. And every barrier you face is, after all, also a potential opportunity.

In John 4, we read the story of Jesus and the woman at the well. Jesus was faced with four barriers when he stopped to talk to her:

1. A moral barrier (she had committed adultery in the eyes of a Jew by taking several husbands)
2. A social barrier (she was a woman; he was a man)
3. A racial barrier (she was a Samaritan and Jesus a Jew, and the two ethnic groups despised each other)
4. A religious barrier (Jews and Samaritans didn't mix on religious grounds)

Yet Jesus addressed her at her point of need, which was greater than the supposed barriers: she was thirsty for living water and he cared enough to break the social taboo and offer it to her. You can trace the way Jesus cut through the barriers, as they spoke and she responded. First, she addressed him as 'Jew'; then, she called Jesus 'Sir'; then, she called him 'prophet'. Finally, she spoke of him as the 'Messiah'.

And as she responded to Jesus with her heart, she couldn't help but tell others the Good News, even though she simply raised a question, 'Come, see a man who told me everything I ever did. Could this be the Christ?' The Bible records, 'Many of the Samaritans from that town believed in him because of the woman's testimony, 'He told me everything I ever did' (John 4:39). Her experience provided her with the opportunity to raise the important question.

Jesus was the friend of sinners, and we need to learn from this. He was comfortable with those who didn't know God, and they with him

– which I think is remarkable. But he wasn't just hanging out having a friendly chat. His friendship compelled him to help them change the way they lived. Jesus even lovingly pointed out to an older, respectable man, Nicodemus, that he was ignorant of 'heavenly things' (John 3:12).

If we are true friends, we will speak the truth in love.

So Where Do We Start?

We might feel guilty about having failed to speak to our friends about the thing we hold most dear. But no feelings of guilt should ever hold us back from starting afresh. And sometimes the best place to start is by saying sorry.

Why not write or phone someone or all of those people on your list and ask if you can talk to them? You could say something like, 'It's only really just occurred to me that we have known each other for a number of years, and I know you know that I am a Christian, but I have never really ever told you about my faith. Would you forgive me? I've always considered you a good friend and it seems so silly, if that's true, that I haven't really explained it to you.'

By actually asking someone to forgive you in the first place, you automatically show that something must have happened in your life. And you are saying, 'I value you.'

The key point is this: How can I care about someone and not share the most important fact in my life? Remember, we are not to preach at them. We are not to give a sermon, but to plant seeds of the grace of God. If we do this generously, the Bible says God is able to water the seed and make it grow.

Action plan! Agree to share the responses you receive to your phone call or initiative during a conversation with a friend.

> How can I care about someone and not share the most important fact in my life?

Sowing Generously

It's crucial, as we set about trying to tell people about the overflow of our heart – the Good News of Jesus – that we don't try to overfeed them. You wouldn't try to feed a leg of chicken to a baby. Instead, you'd take some of the meat, liquidise it and feed it in tiny spoonfuls.

Our job is to sow. God will produce the crop. We must not forget that, ultimately, God is the evangelist. We are called to serve faithfully, not succeed by forcing the issue.

Remember to be interested in the people you're talking to. Have a listening ear to where they are at and what they are really trying to say. They might say, 'I used to go to Sunday school,' 'I was married in church,' or 'Things have been hard since my mum died.'

Don't be afraid to ask what they believe and what involvement they have had with the Christian faith.

Try this:

Think for a few moments about who you could invite around to your home for a drinks evening. Perhaps it's the people in some of your circles. It may, on the other hand, be your next-door neighbours – three to the left, three to the right, and those opposite. Remember, the Gospel spread originally 'from house to house'.

You could plan to do this at a special occasion such as Easter or Christmas. And there's no pressure to force the Gospel down their throat in one go – instead, use the time to get to know them better and genuinely be interested in who they are and what makes them tick.

Simply be prepared to sow one seed: perhaps by giving them an invitation to a carol service or giving them a copy of my booklet *Easter Sonrise* or *More Than a Christmas Carol?* (or something similar) as a gift.

A girl became a Christian through a very timid and shy Christian. At her baptism, in her testimony, the girl said, 'My friend built a bridge from her life to mine – and Christ walked over it.'

Try this:

For the last few minutes, take some time to think about the people whose names you have written in your circles. Pray with two others, offering the names up to God.

End your session by praying the following prayer:

Prayer

Gracious God, thank you for our friends, relatives, work colleagues and acquaintances. Thank you for all the good things they bring to our lives. Thank you for who they are and for who you have created them to be and to become.

Send your Holy Spirit upon us and set our hearts ablaze with love for you, that we might see them through your eyes: with love and compassion. And help us to see afresh the wonderful news that we have for them, that, through Jesus, we have a way back to you. Empower us afresh, that we might minister from the overflow of our hearts.

Please help us to start at home, in our own Jerusalem, by taking the courage to sow seeds of grace in the lives of the people we meet. We pray that you water those seeds through your Spirit and that we might all become like the disciples in those first, daunting days, who stepped out in faith to spread the word that the Messiah has died for us all, so that we all might live. In Jesus' name. Amen.

SESSION 4

THIS IS MY STORY

PART 1: RECAPPING 'WHAT IS FRIENDSHIP EVANGELISM?'

In the previous session we asked, 'What is Friendship Evangelism?' We considered how evangelism starts at home – in the 'Jerusalem' of our own families, friends, neighbours, and work colleagues. We saw that the Gospel, in those first, exciting days of the Early Church, travelled from home to home, and we thought about the people and the homes that we could try to introduce the Gospel to.

We acknowledged that it's very hard to keep quiet about some things in life – like the birth of a new baby, falling in love or our sports team doing well. Jesus was led by compassion and love, and our motivation should be likewise.

Our role in spreading the news is key. Remember that 77 per cent of people come to church because they have been invited by friends or relatives. At the same time, we must not restrict our evangelistic endeavours to inviting people to come to church. We ourselves have to accept the privilege and responsibility of communicating the Good News, not just inviting people to hear the Good News in some other place.

We might feel guilty that we haven't already shared our story with our friends but we shouldn't let that stop us. Instead, we could start with an apology for not having mentioned before, the Good News that has made such a difference to our lives. And from there, we can work at breaking down any barriers by simply spending time with people, inviting them into our home and perhaps offering a simple invitation – to a carol service or something equally non-threatening but inspiring! Our job is to sow seeds; God will water them.

Talking point:

Have you had the opportunity this last week to put these thoughts into action and sow a few seeds? Don't feel guilty if not – but spend a few minutes sharing with each other how you have got on. You might even ask yourselves whether you have missed any opportunities and, if so, what held you back. Discuss what has worked, and what hasn't, and see if you can encourage each other through your own experience.

> We may not be experts, but we all have a story to tell.

PART 2: WE MAY NOT BE EXPERTS, BUT WE ALL HAVE A STORY TO TELL

In today's culture, we like to look for an expert to help us on any given subject. So, if you're expecting a child, for instance, you will seek the advice of a midwife to help you prepare for the birth and subsequent care of your child. However, you'll still ask for advice from your family and friends who have already had a baby – and these people will often share some really useful stories that the midwife, despite her expertise, hasn't told you. Both the expert's information and the friends' anecdotal accounts have a vital role to play in painting a fuller picture.

When we come to sharing our faith, we might think we don't have all the facts and we're not 'expert' enough to break the news about Jesus to other people. It's very easy to focus so hard on what we *don't* know that we forget what we *do* know.

However, we're all very likely to have some wonderful things to say – including stories about the way God works that are unique to us. Our own stories about the role of God in our lives have a key part to play in spreading the Gospel from home to home. They are real, after all, and are rooted in everyday life. They don't come from a textbook but from the heart, and this is often far more likely to speak to someone than a dry and well-rehearsed 'argument'.

Remember, when it comes to telling your story, YOU are the expert!

> Remember, when it comes to telling your story, YOU are the expert!

Don't forget that evangelism is essentially about introducing one person to another – and for that, you need the personal touch. You can win arguments and lose hearts, and you can lose arguments and win hearts. The great thing about 'sharing our story' is that it is a form of evangelism which is very difficult to argue with.

'Jesus Christ has transformed my life' is not a proposition to be disproved, but a statement of faith to be experienced. God entrusted the very first task of spreading the Good News not to university professors but to fishermen.

As we begin to think about how to tell our own stories, it's important to remember that you won't always be able to offer an answer. But that's OK. You will never know it all, and people are usually happy to accept that we don't (in fact, it's a far more honest approach). That said, we mustn't be afraid to do some research. After all, to grow and develop in any new skill we need to be prepared to undergo some training, much the same as we do when we take lessons to learn to drive a car, ski down a mountain or play the piano.

Try this:

Jesus didn't always 'preach' to people. Instead, he identified their need, and often either asked a question or told a story in response. Spend a few minutes looking through your Bible at some of the stories Jesus told. Choose one that speaks to you and note down:

- To whom was Jesus telling the story?

....
....

- What kind of 'props' did he use – characters, plot, description?

....
....

- What was the listener's response, if it is recorded?

....
....

- Why does this story speak to you?

....
....

PART 3: TELLING OUR STORY

The Breaking News of the Gospel needs to be communicated in three parts:

1. **His story**. God's story, from the beginning of creation through to the life, death and resurrection of Jesus.
2. **Your story**. This tells of God coming in power into your life and how this has changed and continues to change you.
3. **Their story**. How God's story relates to the person to whom you are witnessing.

The history of the world is ultimately God's story. When we realise this, and our story (or that of a friend) intersects with God's story, we truly find ourselves in HIStory – the only 'history' that will endure for eternity. (Theologians call this 'salvation history'.)

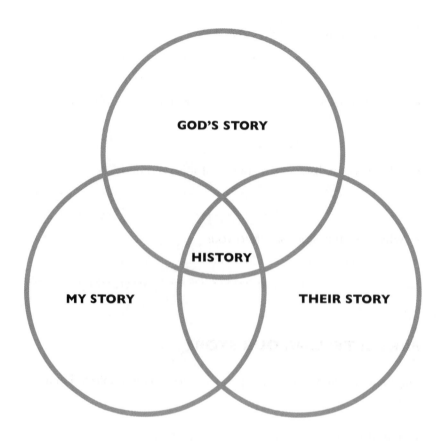

For the rest of this session, we'll focus on your story. Psalm 66:16 says, 'Come and listen, all you who fear God; let me tell you what he has done for me.' When Jesus healed the blind man in John 9, the man said, 'One thing I do know. I was blind but now I see!' (v.25). Then there is the remarkable conclusion to the story of the demon-possessed man who, after Jesus had healed him, begged to be allowed to go with him. But Jesus instructed him, 'Go home to your family and tell them how much the Lord has done for you, and how he has had mercy on you' (Mark 5:19). His witness was likely to be most effective among the people who knew him best. And in Acts

4:20, Peter tells the religious leaders who are trying to keep him quiet, 'we cannot help speaking about what we have seen and heard'.

Winston Churchill once remarked, 'Men occasionally stumble over the truth, but most pick themselves up and hurry off as if nothing had happened.'

The experience of those biblical characters was very different – they had an encounter with the Creator of the cosmos and could not keep quiet. If we have met the same Creator God, we, too, will not be able to keep quiet. In these verses, we find several people who had met with God and couldn't help telling others the story of what happened.

We're *all* called to be witnesses for Jesus – but there's a difference between a witness and a lawyer. A witness simply tells the court what they have experienced. A lawyer, on the other hand, has to plead the case. An 'evangelist' is a bit like a lawyer – but not all of us are called to do this specific task. However, we *are* all called to give an account of what we have seen, heard and experienced of God.

> 'Men occasionally stumble over the truth, but most pick themselves up and hurry off as if nothing had happened.'

Why Do People Receive Christ?

Most of us receive Christ because of either conviction, curiosity or crisis. With either our minds or with our hearts, we realise that we need him. Some of us have simply needed to hang around with Christians to observe and learn about Christ before we are ready to receive him. It is the same with stories of how people came to marry their partner. With some, it was love at first sight, whereas other couples knew each other for a while before they realised the love that had grown between them. It's useful to stop to think about what makes people realise they need Jesus. For some, it's loneliness. To all the lonely people in the world, Jesus offers friendship and love.

But what are the other common problems people face – and what does Jesus have to offer?

Try this:

In the column on the left-hand side, write down some of the common problems that people you know personally are currently facing (e.g. loneliness, fear).

Then write down what Jesus offers and can do for each problem, in the right-hand column.

Common Problems	What Jesus Offers

Once you've finished, spend a few minutes sharing your lists with the rest of the group. You may need more time on your own to think this through more carefully when you get a quiet moment at home. Try to match the problems with incidents in the Gospels where Jesus encounters people with similar challenges.

Most people live their lives in the left-hand column. However, most would *like* to be in the right-hand column. And the good news is, they can. God, through the Holy Spirit, offers so much to us. It's our job to let people know that they can make the transition.

In Galatians 5, we read about the 'fruits of the Spirit'. It's when we are in a relationship with Jesus that his Spirit produces love, joy, peace, patience, kindness, goodness, faithfulness, gentleness and self-control. Put these qualities together and you have a character description of Jesus. As individuals, we each have our strong and weak points. That is why we need to belong to a supportive group of Christians who can fill out the picture and provide a corrective challenge and inspiration for us to deal with the inconsistencies and weaknesses in our character.

Remember that we don't just bring the Breaking News of Jesus. If our lives show evidence of the words in the right-hand column, then we are the Good News. When the eighteenth-century evangelist John Wesley was asked, 'Why do people seem to be drawn to you, almost like a magnet?' he replied, 'When you set yourself on fire, people love to come and see you burn.'

As we display the fruits of the Holy Spirit in our lives or, more accurately, 'fruit' singular, because each of these qualities does not exist in isolation, but as a cluster or like segments of an orange, we demonstrate to others that there is an alternative to life in the left-hand column. But sometimes we need to explain why, and how, that alternative presents itself.

Talking point:

Take a few moments to discuss your lists.

- What have you found helpful in thinking about the Good News in this way?

. . . .

. . . .

- Does it help you feel more confident about what you've got to offer?

  . . . .
  . . . .

- Does it help you to see more clearly, what Jesus has done for you?

  . . . .
  . . . .

- What kinds of 'needs' have you identified?

  . . . .
  . . . .

- And what might you have missed?

  . . . .
  . . . .

PART 4: DIFFERENT KINDS OF TRANSFORMATION STORIES

The tradition of testimony – telling our story of encountering Christ – is as old as the Church itself. When the apostle Paul wrote to the Galatians, he did just this (Galatians 1:13–24).

On this occasion, Paul's story had three sections:

His life before he encountered Christ

> *You have heard of my previous way of life . . . how intensely I persecuted the church of God . . . (v.13)*

How he encountered Christ

> *. . . God, who set me apart from birth . . . was pleased to reveal his Son in me (v.15–16)*

54

His transformation stories since encountering Christ

The churches . . . heard the report: 'The man who formerly persecuted us is now preaching the faith he once tried to destroy'. (v.22–23)

We all have different kinds of transformation stories to tell. And while it's good to get the story right about our conversion, it's important to remember that each time God answers our prayers and does something new in our lives today we've another story to tell.

Your story may not be as sudden and dramatic as that of the apostle Paul. Some people cannot remember a time when they did not love Jesus. For other people, their conversion was a gradual falling in love with Jesus. They cannot remember a specific place and time. If this has been your experience, don't assume that you do not have a testimony to the transforming power of Christ.

Like Paul's, our story should be clear and have distinct sections. If you do not have a dramatic conversion story, your testimony might focus on the influences that led you to Christ and nurtured you, perhaps from a young age. But there will have been moments of revelation and realisation or a growing understanding of what Christ did for you on the Cross and the life to which he called you by the prompting and empowering of the Holy Spirit. A good way to look at it is to break our personal story into four categories:

1. My life before I encountered Christ
2. When I realised I needed Christ
3. How I encountered Christ
4. My life since I encountered Christ

Let's look at each one in turn. Begin to think, as we go through these four areas, of your own story and how it fits into these categories.

> Each time God answers our prayers and does something new in our lives today we've another story to tell.

1: My Life Before I Encountered Christ

We don't all need a 'conversion date' to prove we are Christians. After all, I can't remember the day I was born, but I was – and there seems to be evidence to suggest it!

However your conversion happened, you should give some thought to what your life was like before you followed Christ. How did you act? What were you like as a person? How did you approach life?

MY STORY . . . .
. . . .
. . . .
. . . .
. . . .
. . . .

2: When I Realised I Needed Christ

What helped you turn to Christ? Did you have a particular need from the 'left-hand column' which Jesus met? (Think about things like truth, forgiveness, healing, hope and the promise of eternal life.) Ultimately, we have met a person, not swallowed a doctrine whole. And that's what we really need to communicate as we try to introduce others to the person of Jesus.

MY STORY . . . .
. . . .
. . . .
. . . .
. . . .
. . . .

3: How I Encountered Christ

Where and when did you start your relationship with Jesus? Was it sudden, or gradual? (Don't forget, both are equally valid – so don't be tempted to manipulate your story to make it sound more dramatic. It will resonate with other 'normal people' precisely because it is real, not sensational.) What exactly did you do to become a Christian?

Was there an individual or a number of Christians whose lives made Jesus attractive to you, and what was appealing about their invitation to you to follow their example in committing your life to him?

MY STORY . . . .
. . . .
. . . .
. . . .
. . . .
. . . .

4: My Life Since I Encountered Christ

- What difference has becoming a Christian made to you?
- What are the benefits?
- What has been the cost?
- What are your ongoing struggles?
- From your experience, why would you encourage others to turn to Christ?
- Write down your most recent transformation story.

Remember that for many, this section will prove crucial. The 'proof of the pudding' will be in the living. What authenticates a genuine believer is not so much the 'sinner's prayer' but the 'saint's life'.

MY STORY . . . .
. . . .
. . . .
. . . .
. . . .
. . . .

Don't forget that you're unlikely to need to share the whole of your story at any one time. We must always try to feed people according to their needs – that which is relevant to them at their stage in life. Imagine giving them a segment or two of an orange, not the whole thing. Provoke their curiosity and stimulate their interest, leaving them wanting more. Remember, the most effective evangelism is when the seeker is on the *offensive* ('sorry to bother you, but please tell me why . . .') and the Christian is on the *defensive* ('no that's perfectly OK – I'm happy to tell you why . . .'). The least effective is the other way round. Ensure you stop speaking before they stop listening, then there is the likelihood they will come back for more.

Guidelines to Help You Prepare Your Story

Pray first

The book of James says, 'If any of you lacks wisdom, he should ask God, who gives generously to all' (James 1:5).

Write it down

It says in 1 Peter 3:15, 'Always be prepared to give an answer to everyone who asks you . . .' Don't write pages and pages. Instead, keep it short, so that you can remember it easily. Commit the points to memory – a rough-and-ready witness from the heart will be more effective than a stilted and polished performance.

Write out two versions: a 3-minute version and a 10-minute version. Edit out any theological language or religious jargon. Ask a Christian friend to read it through and ask them if it is clear and true to the person they know you to be. You might also want to ask a friend who is not yet a follower of Jesus to read it for their comments. Read it aloud to yourself until you are thoroughly familiar with it.

Be gentle and respect the person you're talking to

That same verse in Peter goes on to say, 'But do this with gentleness and respect.'

Avoid negative remarks about other religions and denominations. We don't ever need to put other religions down in order to lift Jesus up. (Of course, if people ask you about other religions, try to help them, constructively, to see where the Christian faith differs and what that might mean for them.)

We show respect by listening carefully to what they say and by observing and interpreting their body language.

Share, don't preach

Unlike in a sermon, you are sharing your experience. Remember you are the 'Witness' not the 'Lawyer'. Make it shamelessly experiential. Genuine sharing means being honest, vulnerable and open to the responses that our story may evoke. God is not glorified by exaggeration or selective truth telling. What we say must ring true.

Make use of the Bible

'For the word of God,' Hebrews 4:12 says, 'is living and active. Sharper than any double-edged sword.' However, don't be a Bible-basher! Once again, feed people according to their needs, not according to how much scripture you can stuff down their throats! Sometimes it is preferable to base what you have to say on just one verse or passage of the Gospel. You might want to keep a few copies of the New Testament to give away after having shared a verse or story, leaving a marker in the page.

Make it real

Don't be tempted to hype it up or be embarrassed of a seemingly undramatic conversion story. Tell it as it is and God will use it. Remember, your story may seem ordinary to you because it is so familiar but it may be strikingly fresh to the person with whom you are sharing.

Don't lapse into religious clichés

We all tend to speak in Christian jargon from time to time, but remember that people who haven't been to church won't know what you're talking about if you do. We have to keep it simple. In 1 Corinthians 2:1 Paul says, 'When I came to you . . . I did not come to you with eloquence or superior wisdom as I proclaimed to you the testimony about God.'

Try this:

Provide a paraphrase for the following terms:

Salvation:. . . . .
Redemption:. . . . .
Grace:. . . . .
Sin:. . . . .
Born Again:. . . . .

Other words or phrases associated with the Gospel:
. . . .
. . . .

Compare your paraphrases with those suggested by other people in your group.

Make it Christ-centred

Does your story give glory to Christ? Remember, Christ is the King of Kings – you need to use your story to point to him. Inevitably, your testimony focuses on your experience, but it must always point away from you to the Lord Jesus who makes it all possible.

Keep it short and to the point

You're not preaching a sermon at church; you're sharing your story – the kind of Breaking News that you can't help sharing with others.

Writing it out provides a helpful discipline for you to review what you are saying. Revisit it from time to time to ensure that it is still current and to check whether it expresses your deepening understanding of the Gospel.

Try this:

Spend a few minutes digesting these guidelines, then pray and ask God to help you as you think about your story. Then rewrite an edited version taking into account the four categories we looked at earlier. We can always improve our first attempt.

Once you've finished – you shouldn't take much longer than five minutes at this stage – try sharing your story with the person sitting next to you. Think of them as someone totally new to the Good News you're trying to communicate. Once you've finished, swap roles and listen to the other person's story as if you are hearing 'Breaking News'. Then link up with another two people and each share with the group of four, the story you heard from your partner. This will test your ability to listen, and also help the person whose story you are repeating by revealing to them how much they remembered, what they found most significant, and what they misunderstood!

End your session by praying this prayer:

A Prayer

Lord Jesus Christ, thank you that you came to live among us, to bring God's story. Thank you that as our story intersects with your story we find ourselves in eternal History. We offer our stories to you, and ask that you would help us to communicate these effectively to those around us – understanding that it's our lives that are the living, breathing evidence of the Breaking News of the Kingdom of God. We also pray for everyone who will hear the story in the weeks, months and years to come, and we ask that you would go before us to prepare them for what we have to say. In your name. Amen.

SESSION 5

DEMONSTRATING THE GOOD NEWS

PART 1: RECAPPING 'THIS IS MY STORY'

Last time, we asked, 'How can I share my story?' Perhaps few of us are 'expert' evangelists, but the good news is that we do, nonetheless, have a story to tell. And we're compelled to tell it – not just because the Bible says so, but also because no one can keep Good News to themselves.

We also saw that Jesus didn't just preach to people; he engaged with them – by identifying their needs and then asking a question or telling a story in response.

What kind of needs should we try to identify? We wrote down in one column some of the common problems people face. And then we wrote down what Jesus offers in return for each problem in the opposite column and asked how we could take people from the left-hand column to the right-hand column.

Finally, we thought about the personal story we have to tell and broke it into four parts:

1. My life before I encountered Christ
2. When I realised I needed Christ
3. How I encountered Christ
4. My life since I encountered Christ

Talking point:

- Have you had an opportunity to share your story this week? If so, reflect for a few minutes upon what worked and what didn't.
  ....
  ....

- What did you learn from the experience?
  ....
  ....

- Do you need to hone the way you told it – or the elements you've included – now that you've tried it out?
  ....
  ....

If you haven't told your story, don't feel guilty. There will be many more opportunities in the future. Ask the group members to pray that the Lord will give you wisdom and boldness.

PART 2: SOCIAL JUSTICE AND EVANGELISM

Try this:

Who is my neighbour?

At the time of writing, I have just returned from a visit to Kenya with the charity Compassion. During the visit, we visited Kiberia, a slum township outside Nairobi with a population of over half a million. Kiberia has no proper roads, no sewerage system, no running water or electricity. HIV is rampant and these conditions combined with entrenched poverty and widespread unemployment have made the township particularly conducive to the spread of disease.

During the visit, my assistant, Chris Moffat, commented that this situation would not be tolerated if this were a suburb of London, so why do we tolerate it merely because of the separation of miles? Such situations bring into sharp focus the question that the parable of the Good Samaritan would prompt us to ask, 'Who is my neighbour?'

Read together Luke 10:25–37 (the parable of the Good Samaritan). When you've finished, discuss, for a few moments, the following:

- In the 'global village', who is my neighbour?

....

....

- What pressures do we, as citizens of the twenty-first century, face as we seek to answer this question with integrity?

....

....

(NB: There is no right or wrong answer to this, as such. As the world changes around us, it's up to us as Christians to respond by asking the old questions again within our new contexts.)

In this session, we will focus on social justice and evangelism. There is a tendency to split the two, in our minds, into separate compartments. However, as we shall see in this session, from the perspective of the Bible both properly belong together. The demonstration and proclamation of the Gospel are two sides of the same coin.

We must resist the temptation to separate Gospel words from Gospel works. Editions of the New Testament that print the words of Christ in red may tempt us to do this!

Social justice, like evangelism, isn't something we can leave to the so-called 'experts'. And that's because it is, in fact, a fundamental part of the Breaking News of Jesus Christ, which we all have the responsibility of sharing. Social justice is embedded in the very message itself. God is on the side of those who have no one else to help them. And so our words must always be matched by our actions. Remember, we are not only to speak the Good News; we are to be the Good News. We must never allow a separation between lip and life, between proclamation and demonstration. We cannot be authentic disciples of Jesus if we fail to show the compassion of Jesus.

It is true that some within the Church will have a particular calling to either the demonstration or proclamation of the Gospel and this will find expression in passion and gifting.

But this is not a licence to let the rest of us off the hook. Such people are to be 'prophetic irritants' in the body of Christ, provoking each one of us to play our part. Jesus said (in Matthew 25:37–40):

> *'Then the righteous will answer him, "Lord, when did we see you hungry and feed you, or thirsty and give you something to drink? When did we see you a stranger and invite you in, or needing clothes and clothe you? When did we see you sick or in prison and go to visit you?"*
>
> *'The King will reply, "I tell you the truth, whatever you did for one of the least of these . . . you did for me".'*

As Christians, then, we are called to struggle against everything that condemns people to a sub-human existence – such as hunger, disease, poverty, inequality, exploitation, abuse and injustice. The struggle itself tells a story about the God we serve.

When the BBC presented a series based on a popular survey *The 100 Greatest Britons* it was interesting to note which Christians made it into the list: John Wesley, William Wilberforce, William Booth and Florence Nightingale.

Also, when an international research organization carried out a worldwide survey on 'leaders who made a difference and whom you could not ignore', Mother Teresa came first and Archbishop Desmond Tutu second. All these people were characterised and compelled by

---

Our words must always be matched by our actions. We are not only to speak the Good News; we are to be the Good News.

a faith in Christ that was demonstrated in social action. Compassion and justice is a language the world understands and is deeply evangelistic. People can argue against proclamation, but cannot ignore a demonstration of the love of God.

During the Clinton administration in the USA, Mother Teresa was awarded the Congressional medal for her humanitarian service. Instead of accepting the medal in silence, the elderly and brave nun took the opportunity to criticise the Clinton administration on its policy on abortion. Shortly afterwards a journalist interviewed President Clinton and asked him what he thought of the criticisms levelled at him by Mother Teresa. There was a pause. 'It's very difficult to argue with a life so beautifully lived.'

Try this:

Jesus said, 'Blessed are you who are poor.'

- But what do we mean when we speak of 'the poor' today?
  . . . .
  . . . .

- Who are they?
  . . . .
  . . . .

- Where are they?
  . . . .
  . . . .

- What immediately springs to your mind?
  . . . .
  . . . .

- Write down your initial thoughts on Jesus' statement.

. . . .

. . . .

Now read Deuteronomy 15:4–5 and 7–11, and afterwards discuss the passage. To the extent that this 'year of Jubilee' was practised by Israel, it would provide a challenge and inspiration to the world at large. Unfortunately, there is no evidence of this 'setting things straight' once every 50 years being implemented in ancient Israel.

Once you've finished, spend a few moments in silence, before praying:

> God our Father, thank you for sending your Son to live with us and to show us how to live. Please help us to understand that the Good News is not just words, but also words in action – the practical outpouring of your love to anyone who needs it. Please give us the courage and strength to begin to change, if not the whole world, then the world around us. Amen.

Please give us the courage and strength to begin to change, if not the whole world, then the world around us. Amen.

PART 3: THE BIBLE AND THE POOR

It's easy to see poverty as a self-inflicted wound – as something that the poor could have avoided through a bit more effort, some better management and a bit more luck. In our economic system, we've become used to the idea that the talented and hard-working people are duly rewarded, while the unlucky and the lazy ones also get what they deserve – nothing.

But that's not how the Bible sees it.

It may feel as if the poor have always been around but that's not the case. In fact, the book of Genesis doesn't mention the word 'poor' at all. It wasn't part of the original plan or indeed the natural order. In

Abraham's time, if one person was rich, the whole tribe was rich, because wealth belonged to the tribe, not the individual.

Sadly, the sharing spirit didn't last forever. As the world 'developed', some became richer, while others grew poorer. The story of God's involvement in human history – that starts in the Old Testament and proceeds into the New – is saturated with references to the poor. God clearly cares deeply about the fact that some have more than enough, while others have nothing, and the advance of his kingdom is intrinsically linked with the liberation and salvation of the poor from their practical 'captivity', as much as any spiritual bondage. The world has enough for everyone's 'need' but not everyone's 'greed'.

In Jesus' day, poverty was widespread due to the crushing burden of taxation imposed by the Romans. People fled their homes when it became known that the tax gatherer was in the area. Also, subsistence farming meant that people faced not only starvation but also economic ruin when their harvests failed.

What Does the Bible Say?

The Old Testament uses several different words to describe 'the poor'. 'Ani' is the most common word for 'poor' (occurring 77 times). It means 'a person who is bowed down' – the 'ani' has to look up to others on whom they're dependent – and is contrasted not, as you might expect, with the 'rich', but with the 'oppressor' who keeps them in their place. 'Anaw' is used 18 times and refers to people who feel they have little worth before God. The word 'ebyon', meanwhile, is used 60 times to refer to the situation of beggars.

These three words are charged with emotion – they're not neutral or simply descriptive. All of them are a call for urgent change. When we think about the poor, let's be careful not to lump everyone into the same, generic category. Hopefully, this biblical distinction helps us to think more compassionately about people who have little – and more critically of those of us who maintain the status quo (even if it's just through our own inactivity).

One role the Church can have is to challenge this 'status quo' – but when we do, let's not expect popularity.

The South American Roman Catholic Bishop, Helda Camera, once said, 'When I feed the hungry, they call me a saint – when I ask, "Why are they hungry", they call me a communist.'

The New Testament continues to record God's compassion for the poor, with many references to the social conditions of the time. We read about landowners, tax collectors, labourers, slaves, honest and dishonest stewards, unjust judges and widows who plead for their rights.

The Bible doesn't just describe poverty in terms of money but in terms of power. The most common Greek word for 'poor' in the New Testament is *'ptochos'*, which means 'to duck away in fear'. But the Bible suggests that God – the all-powerful – took upon himself 'the very nature of a servant' (Philippians 2:7) in order to turn the power structures of the world upside down and show us a better way – a way of justice, which brings peace and casts out all fear.

'Justice' is the opposite of 'just us'; it should never be 'just us'. To be a Christian is to become open to the rest of the world, not as a master but as a servant.

It's not that the poor are especially good people, while the rich are especially evil. God is on the side of the poor *because no one else is*. And that means that we should be, too. In all of our relationships, we can choose: to maintain power or to help to break it down; to maintain oppressive systems or to end them; to maintain the status quo (which serves us very nicely, thank you) or to fight for those who will otherwise forever be without power, food, money, and possibilities.

Talking point:

Dr Robert Lupton is a psychiatrist who works with deprived people in an inner-city context. He has a friend called Mrs Smith, who he describes below. Read this section together, and then discuss the questions that follow.

> Mrs Smith is 66. She has some mental health issues, is badly overweight, twice a great-grandmother and a devoted member of our church. Though she must live with her extended family in a deplorable, overcrowded house, her buoyant spirit is undaunted.
>
> 'You're my buddy,' she'll say to me with a broad, snaggletooth grin. 'I pray for you every day.' And then she'll give me a long bear hug. She wants to sit with me in every service and, even though the smell of stale sweat and excrement is often nauseating, I am pleased to have Mrs Smith by my side.
>
> She has often hinted – sometimes blatantly – that she would like to come home with us for a little visit. Nothing would delight her more than to have Sunday dinner with us.
>
> But there is a conflict. It has to do with the values which my wife and I learned from our childhood. We have always believed it is good stewardship to take care of our belongings, treat them with respect and get long service from them.
>
> To invite Mrs Smith into our home means having filth and stench soil our things, stains on my settee and offensive odours in our living room. Unknowingly, she forces upon me a conflict, a clashing of values inside me.
>
> 'Preserve and maintain, conserve and protect . . .' the words of an ethic that has served us well. And subtly, over time, these values of our culture have filtered into our theology until they have become part of it.
>
> It is increasingly difficult to separate the values of achievement from the values of the kingdom. I thank God for Mrs Smith and

the conflict she brings me. In her, more clearly than in sermons, do I encounter the Christ of scripture saying, 'whatever you did for the least of these . . . you did for me'.

- How do you react to this account?

  . . . .

  . . . .

- Do you know of any Mrs Smiths yourself?

  . . . .

  . . . .

- What value do you place on your possessions – your carpets, your sofas, your material goods?

  . . . .

  . . . .

- Is your ethic to preserve and maintain?

  . . . .

  . . . .

- And if so, what can we all do to change our attitude?

  . . . .

  . . . .

PART 4: ACTIONS SPEAK LOUDER THAN WORDS

Sometimes, the most important things we *say* are the things that we *do* for people such as being concerned about the concerns of others, loving and caring for those who are unlike us and helping the marginalised and powerless. It is in doing these things that we become true witnesses and evangelists.

Social justice can go before evangelism in the sense that it can open closed doors, break down prejudice and become a bridge over which the Gospel can pass.

It has been said; people don't care how much we know, until they know how much we care.

However, we do not engage in social action as a means to evangelism, because that would introduce an ulterior motive or even make the help conditional on the person's eventual acceptance of the Gospel. Loving acts are unconditional, neither demanding nor expecting in return.

Yet, even if we don't manage to create that bridge, we must act with a social conscience regardless; for, as Titus writes (2:14), one of the reasons Christ gave himself for us was 'to purify for himself a people that are his very own, eager to do what is good.'

Put another way, the book of James (2:14) says, 'Dear brothers and sisters, what's the use of saying you have faith, if you don't prove it by your actions? That kind of faith can't save anyone' (NLT).

It isn't enough either just to have faith or, as budding evangelists, just to talk about faith; for (as James writes in James 2:17) 'faith by itself, if it is not accompanied by action, is dead'. The Breaking News of Christ is that hope has broken into our hopeless world – this has radical and practical implications for us all. Faith in Christ entails exercising trust in him on a daily basis in every area of life. If we are not prepared to trust him in this way, then we are in no position to encourage others to put their faith in Christ.

> Sometimes, the most important things we *say* are the things that we *do*.

Try this:

What are we already doing – as individuals, as a home-group, as a church – to ensure that our faith finds expression in social justice? Spend a few minutes writing a list.

> There is no competition between lighthouse keepers and lifeboat savers.

. . . .
. . . .
. . . .
. . . .
. . . .

Now brainstorm the possibilities for doing more – for working with the poor as individuals, as a home-group and as a church. Don't, at this stage, discuss whether an idea is good, or whether it's practical or not. Every idea is a possibility, so list them all, and begin to group them into categories (such as the bereaved, the homeless, those in prison, the poor in developing countries and so on).

. . . .
. . . .
. . . .
. . . .
. . . .

We should never separate words, works and wonders. After all, there is no competition between lighthouse keepers and lifeboat savers.

And we must not forget that those things we do *for* God we must also do *with* God. Mother Teresa once said of her work in Calcutta:

> We try to pray through our work by doing it with Jesus, for Jesus, to Jesus. That helps us to put our whole heart and soul into doing it. The dying, the crippled, the mentally ill, the unwanted, the unloved – they are Jesus in disguise.

As we contemplate ways in which we can demonstrate the Gospel, it is easy to be overwhelmed by the enormous need all around us.

Consider the story of the couple walking along a beach throwing stranded starfish back into the sea. A passer-by commented on the futility of their actions: 'What difference are you making? There are thousands of starfish on this beach alone.' One of the couple responded with starfish in hand, 'It means everything to this one.'

We've much to do and little time to do it. No one person can change the world, but we can all change the world for one person. And that's an amazing possibility and privilege. As the eighteenth-century philosopher Edmund Burke wrote, 'Nobody made a greater mistake than he who did nothing because he could only do a little.'

> 'Nobody made a greater mistake than he who did nothing because he could only do a little.'

Archbishop Desmond Tutu gave this advice to an enquirer who was faced with the temptation of the paralysis of analysis: 'How do you eat an elephant? . . . One chunk at a time!' When it comes to our committee deliberations, we often have to confess that when all is said and done, a lot more is said than done!

We returned from our Compassion trip to Kenya both shocked and stirred but also encouraged to see how Compassion's child sponsorship programme has transformed the lives of thousands. One highlight from the trip was to have a meal with four University students whose lives have been transformed from their slum environments since Compassion started to look after them. Why not prayerfully consider sponsoring a child with Compassion. (For further information, see Appendix 2.)

The prayer of St Francis of Assisi seems so appropriate:

A Prayer

Lord, make us instruments of your peace.
Where there is hatred, let us now love;
Where there is injury, pardon;
Where there is discord, union;
Where there is doubt, faith;
Where there is despair, hope;
Where there is darkness, light;
Where there is sadness, joy.
Grant that we may not so much seek to be consoled
   as to console;
To be understood as to understand;
To be loved as to love.
For it is in giving that we receive;
It is in pardoning that we are pardoned;
And it is in dying that we are born to eternal life.
Amen.

SESSION 6

HOW CAN WE RECEIVE POWER FOR EVANGELISM?

For this session, each group will need a candle, matches and a balloon.

PART I: DEMONSTRATING THE GOOD NEWS

In the last session, we looked at the crucial role of social justice in evangelism. We acknowledged that it is a fundamental part of the Breaking News of Jesus Christ that we all have the responsibility of sharing.

We asked, 'Who are the poor?' and looked at what the Bible has to say. The different words the Bible uses for 'the poor' are charged with emotion – and they call for urgent change. 'Justice' is the opposite of 'just us'; and to be a Christian is to become open to the rest of the world, not as a master, but as a servant.

Sometimes, the most important things we *say* are the things that we *do* for people. As the book of James (2:14) observes, 'Dear brothers and sisters, what's the use of saying you have faith if you don't prove it by your actions? That kind of faith can't save anyone' (NLT).

Talking point:

- Now you've had time to reflect on the role of social justice and evangelism, what did you find challenging or inspiring about the previous session?

. . . .

. . . .

- And what have you decided to do about it?

. . . .

. . . .

- Share your ideas before you move on.

. . . .

. . . .

PART 2: POWER FOR A PURPOSE

In this final session, we will ask, 'How can we receive power for evangelism?'

The story written by Luke in the book of Acts that records how the disciples received the Holy Spirit is both exciting and fascinating. It's about real people in a real-life situation, like you and me today. Luke's message is simply this: that the Spirit of God is doing *his* thing in the midst of a world intent on doing *its* thing. He records the acts of the Holy Spirit through the Acts of the Apostles.

The word 'Pentecost' literally means 'fiftieth'. When God sent his Spirit upon the disciples in the upper room, it was the fiftieth day after Passover (the annual celebration of that great moment in Israel's history when they were delivered by God from captivity in Egypt). The disciples received power, which took them out onto the streets of Jerusalem to spread the Good News, and then way beyond . . .

The book of Acts, which records what happened next, is jam-packed with both talk and action. There are riots, demonstrations, arrests, shipwreck, humour . . . all of which is, in fact, incidental to the real action that threads its way throughout these events.

And that golden thread is evangelism – the Breaking News of Jesus Christ. Purely and simply, Acts is about spreading this Breaking News and about how we must depend on the power of the Spirit to make the news real and relevant to all who hear it.

> We must depend on the power of the Spirit to make the news real and relevant to all who hear it.

The question is, 'What can we learn from the activity of the Holy Spirit in the book of Acts?' Jesus promised, 'You will receive power when the Holy Spirit comes on you' (Acts 1:8). In this session, we will explore what that means for the earliest followers of Jesus, and for those of us today who follow in their footsteps.

Try this:

Imagine, for a moment, that you are with the disciples on the day of Pentecost. It's been a bewildering time – the man you've followed for three years was crucified, and it seemed the world had collapsed around you. Then, astonishingly, on the third day he appeared to you. And for the next 40 days, he appeared when he was least expected: on the shore after a fishing trip; on the road to Emmaus; through the walls of the upper room where you were huddled together in fear. Now you've seen him ascend to heaven with your own eyes. But you don't know what's next. He's promised to send his Spirit – but what does that mean?

Think about how you feel, as you wait.

• What does the room smell like?

. . . .

. . . .

- What is written on the faces of your brothers and sisters around you?

  . . . .

  . . . .

- What are you talking about?

  . . . .

  . . . .

God empowers us for a purpose.

- How is the mood?

  . . . .

  . . . .

Write down your feelings and observations, or just keep imagining. Try as hard as you can to picture the mood and sense the atmosphere after Jesus' ascension and before the arrival of the Holy Spirit.

When you've done that, read Acts 2:1–4 and spend a few moments in silence, imagining the scene. So this is what Jesus promised. It's happening as he said it would. Where do we go from here?

Jesus promises in Acts 1:8 that 'you will receive power when the Holy Spirit comes on you'. But why? Pentecost is not only about God's saving grace, bringing the application of salvation to our lives; nor is it simply an ethical event, designed to help transform our character. It is also a *missiological* event, propelling us out to share the Breaking News of Christ.

That is why Jesus continues this statement by saying, 'you will be my witnesses in Jerusalem, and in all Judea and Samaria, and to the ends of the earth' (Acts 1:8).

In the New Testament, there is a connection between being FILLED UP, CHARGED UP and SENT OUT.

God empowers us for a purpose. God's Holy Spirit not only helps us to know Christ, but also helps us to make Christ known.

First Fruits

Pentecost was also called the Feast of the First Fruits; it was the time at which the first ripe corn was offered to God. And in Acts 2, we see the 'first fruits' of the harvest of the Gospel – a harvest that is still being gathered all over the world today.

So when the Spirit came at Pentecost they all became witnesses! The Spirit is the moving power, energy, inspiration and strength behind *all* evangelism.

The Holy Spirit guides us and equips us. And the Holy Spirit alone can bring conviction and faith to people who don't know Jesus. Our part is to be the messenger. So without the Spirit we labour in vain.

(At this point, your group will need the candle, matches and a balloon.)

Try this:

One person is to read out the meditation whilst another follows the directions:

> We have noted that Jesus said to his disciples, 'You will receive POWER when the Holy Spirit comes on you' (Acts 1:8).
>
> The Greek word for power is DUNAMIS – from which we get the English word DYNAMITE.
>
> We read in Acts 2:1–4 that the Holy Spirit fell like WIND and FIRE.
>
> FIRE purifies and signifies the HOLINESS the Spirit brings.
>
> *(At this point, one member takes the matches and lights the candle.)*

81

WIND stands for the BREATH of God – we can't see it, but can see HIS effect in our lives. As Luke is emphasising the empowering of the Holy Spirit for mission rather than personal holiness, he describes the coming of the Holy Spirit not as a 'gentle breath from heaven' but as 'a violent wind'.

(One person now blows up the balloon. We can't see the person's breath but can see the effects.)

The wind and fire of God together give the power of God to witness to the GOOD NEWS of GOD. Any firefighter will tell you that wind and fire make for an unstoppable combination.

(Here a person puts the inflated balloon on the naked flame until it explodes!)

DYNAMITE!

PART 3: SIX WAYS THE SPIRIT HELPS US

1. By Calling Us to Be a Missionary

What me? A missionary? That's right! From a New Testament perspective, all Christians are called to be missionaries. The question is, 'In what capacity am I called?'

Remember, a missionary is not a person who crosses the sea, but a person who sees the Cross. When you have seen the Cross, the love of Christ compels you.

The book of Acts provides us with two spheres or capacities for being a missionary, which are very helpful. And the good news is that the Holy Spirit can help us to discern which we are called to be.

First, there are the 'WORKPLACE' missionaries, like the Apostles who remained in Jerusalem after Pentecost (Acts 8:1). For most

Christians, their primary missionary sphere is their place of work. Remember that the household in the New Testament was a place of business and social contact.

Second, there are 'WANDERING' missionaries like Paul, Barnabas and Philip (Acts 8:4). These tend to be Christians who have a primary gifting in evangelism, preaching and teaching the Gospel, and would include itinerant evangelists (like me) and cross-cultural mission partners.

We need both types of missionaries in today's world. And as we try to discern which type we might be, the Holy Spirit will help to guide us, because the Spirit is the driving force behind all of our evangelism.

> Prayer is crucial if we wish to evangelise effectively.

2. Prayer

Prayer is crucial if we wish to evangelise effectively. It's oxygen for the holy fire. The New Testament itself is soaked in references to prayer. In fact, it knows no evangelism without prayer, and no prayer that does not lead to evangelism. Luke, in his gospel, relates everything to prayer – not that prayer is everything, but, rather, that everything is prayer.

Jesus, our ultimate model, always prayed before he acted. 'The harvest is plentiful,' he said in Matthew 9:37–38, 'but the workers are few. Ask the Lord of the harvest, therefore, to send out workers into his harvest field.'

It was in the upper room, while Jesus was with his disciples partaking in the Last Supper that Jesus' longest recorded prayer is found. He prayed for himself, for the completion of his own mission. Then he prayed for his disciples, 'As you sent me into the world, I have sent them into the world' (John 17:18). And then Jesus prays for all who will believe in him through their message.

His prayer life motivated others to pray. We read that, in that famous upper room in Jerusalem, the disciples 'all joined together constantly in prayer, along with the women and Mary the mother of Jesus, and with his brothers' (Acts 1:14).

As John Wesley said, 'God does nothing but in answer to prayer.' It's not just that prayer can launch a spiritual awakening; prayer can turn out to *be* the awakening itself. And today, churches that experience revival are those that are characterised by prayer.

If we want to work for God, we should form a committee – but God so loved the world that he did not send a committee! However, if we want to work *with* God, we should pray. As the apostle Paul wrote, 'I urge you . . . by our Lord Jesus Christ and by the love of the Spirit, to join me in my struggle by praying to God for me' (Romans 15:30).

> We should pray because we cannot achieve anything through clever plans alone... prayer is one of the spiritual weapons God has given us, and unused weapons do not win wars.

We should pray because we cannot achieve anything through clever plans alone, but through the work of the Holy Spirit. It is crucial that we mobilise prayer in order to evangelise, for prayer is one of the spiritual weapons God has given us, and unused weapons do not win wars.

When we pray, we get involved in missionary work. But it's important that we try to see prayer not just as something we do on Sundays at church or Wednesday nights at a home group, but to see it, instead, as a way of life, something that permeates and infuses our journey.

What should be the content of our prayers?

The Bible calls us to pray more for those who are conveying the Breaking News of Jesus Christ than those who are receiving it. That's because conversion is, ultimately, the work of the Holy Spirit. It's the messengers who need God's help.

We're instructed to pray into five basic areas:

1. Pioneers: for workers to be sent to the mission field (Matthew 9:38)
2. Planning: for guidance – for who to send and where to go (Acts 13:2–3)
3. Productivity: for the success of the message (Acts 4:29–31)
4. Protection: for protection and help for missionaries and all who witness (Psalm 5:11)
5. Persecutors: for our enemies and persecutors. Jesus leads the way by asking his Father to forgive those who are crucifying him (Matthew 5:44).

And what form should they take?

Prayer can take many different forms. It doesn't just have to be a set of written or spoken words. As you try to make prayer a way of life, think creatively about how you can pray in different ways, and at different times. I like to walk and pray. Others enjoy using the arts as a means of praying.

Talking point:

Take a moment to reflect on your church and personal prayer life.

• Can any changes and improvements be made to develop your prayer life in relation to evangelism?

. . . .

. . . .

• Can you pray in different ways?

. . . .

. . . .

- Share your experiences and thoughts before moving on.

. . . .

. . . .

3. The Spirit Helps Us in Personal Evangelism

As we try to spread the Breaking News of Christ to others, it's important to remain attuned to the Holy Spirit, who not only brings us power and confidence, but also guidance.

Sometimes God can ask us to perform a specific task. In Acts 8:26–40, we read the story of Philip and the Ethiopian eunuch. Philip acts on the prompting he gets to go and run alongside the chariot of the Ethiopian. From there, he is able to take the opportunity God has given, to speak the Good News to this man.

The Holy Spirit will sometimes guide us in a similar way. But it's up to us to be listening out for his promptings, and then – just as important – to act upon them. Think carefully, however, about the way you go about this. If you believe that God is telling you to pray for someone's healing, ask them if you can pray for them. But don't tie yourself – or God – down by saying that God is going to heal them. Allow God to work through you, as you act in obedience to his still, small voice. God answers prayers in different ways at different times – the secret is to never stop praying.

4. The Spirit Gives Direction in Church Evangelism

In Acts 16, Paul and his team experience all sorts of frustrations. Doors seem to be closing in their faces, rather than opening. Their plans seem to be thwarted at every turn. But it turns out to be the work of the Holy Spirit.

They had to learn to 'die' to their own plans for the sake of God's plans; to die to their own timetable, in order to live by God's. And when they do, in Acts 16, we see God opening up an amazing new door into Europe for them.

The Lord may shut doors before he guides us to the one he has opened.

It's not that we shouldn't make our own plans and be creative and diligent about how we try to spread the Gospel; God wants us to take the initiative. But sometimes, he has a different plan, so we must be patient and sensitive to the calling of the Holy Spirit, as we pursue the path he wants us to travel.

For example, a number of churches have discovered that certain areas of their local communities are more receptive to the Gospel than others. Clearly, this doesn't mean that we don't keep trying in the tougher, barren areas, but it does mean we should pray about where God wants us to focus our efforts. It might be in one place or group in particular, such as children, the elderly, single parents, and so on . . .

When the Spirit is moving, expect and prepare for new life to spring up.

Try this:

Think about your own locality and the area your church seeks to serve.

- Where has the Gospel been received effectively and enthusiastically?
  . . . .
  . . . .

- Where has it fallen on hard ground?
  . . . .
  . . . .

After thinking about this for a few moments and discussing it, spend a few quiet minutes listening to God, to see if he is directing your thoughts towards any region or area in particular. If you sense strongly that God is directing you, make a note, and let your church leadership know.

End this session by praying for the barren places you have talked about.

5. The Spirit Helps Us to Witness Through Word, Works and Wonders

In our last session, we saw how God empowers us to communicate his love through works as well as word; social action as well as proclamation. The third 'w' is 'wonders'.

The first Christians regularly saw healing and 'deliverance' as part of their evangelism. When Jesus sent out his mission teams, we are told, 'he gave them power and authority to drive out all demons and to cure diseases, and he sent them out to preach the kingdom of God and to heal the sick' (Luke 9:1–2).

So it was only natural that the disciples should do likewise. They were, after all, following in his footsteps. In Acts 3:1–10 and Acts 19:11–16 we see that God loves the world so much that he wants to bring healing and deliverance from all kinds of bondage.

I believe we should seek insight and wisdom from God to be prophetic in our evangelism. As I have sought God as to how I should pray for a person who is sick, or speak to someone who is not yet a Christian, the Lord has given me insight and wisdom to know how to pray and to speak a word into someone's life that dramatically transforms them.

I recommend everyone to read Dr Mark Stibbe's book *Prophetic Evangelism* and learn the theology and practice of this. (For more information, see Bibliography.)

6. The Spirit Helps Us to Understand Spiritual Warfare

We often look at the world and think that there's little we can do to change it. But the Holy Spirit helps us to see things the way God sees them. And that changes everything.

In the Old Testament, the prophet Joel prophesied that God would pour his Spirit out upon all people. And this outpouring would be characterised by a release of prophecy and vision – in other words, God would help us to see things from heaven's point of view.

That involves acknowledging that there are what we call 'principalities and powers' at work (Ephesians 6) – forces which are trying to bring evil to reign, and to thwart our attempts to spread the Good News across the world.

Thomas McAlpine wrote a fascinating study called *Facing the Powers* (see Bibliography), and in his foreword, he wrote:

> All over the world, folk in missions are beginning to recognise that the biblical language about principalities and powers cannot be dismissed as first-century, pre-scientific superstition. The world of spirits and the supernatural is real and has its impact on mission.
>
> Sadly, we in the West are ill-equipped to think with clarity and depth because our dominant Enlightenment [worldview] has no space for this level of reality.

It's important that we discern the strategies of the devil and his demonic army. Satan even ended up thwarting the apostle Paul at times (see 1 Thessalonians 2:18) – so we should not be surprised if we encounter such resistance.

That's not to say we should be afraid or focus unduly on the power of Satan. Paul reminds us to 'put on the full armour of God, so that when the day of evil comes, you may be able to stand your ground' (Ephesians 6:13).

89

We can put on the belt of truth, the breastplate of righteousness, and have 'feet fitted with the readiness that comes from the gospel of peace'. There's also the shield of faith and the helmet of salvation. It's important that we put on this armour, day by day. Try to think, perhaps when you are getting dressed in the morning, of putting on this additional spiritual armour.

Paul instructs us to put on 'the full armour of God'.

Try this:

Before we move on to the conclusion, read together Ephesians 6:10–18. Think, for a few minutes, about what each of the elements of the armour of God means, and how they can help you. Write this list on a card and place it somewhere that can remind you daily to put on the armour of God.

- Belt of Truth
- Breastplate of Righteousness
- Shoes of the Gospel of Peace
- Shield of Faith
- Helmet of Salvation
- Sword of the Spirit

Paul instructs us to put on 'the full armour of God'. From the above list, are there any pieces that you are prone to overlook? What have been the consequences? Resolve not to overlook them in the future.

PART 4: CONCLUDING REMARKS

The book of Acts, written by Luke, is all about spreading the Breaking News of Jesus Christ. It does not, however, sanction any one method. The apostles used every way they could think of to get the word out.

The only model is 'saturation' evangelism. We must be similarly open to any ideas, and to new ideas, as we seek to express the transforming Good News of Christ to a dying world.

We may be 'only' human but, thankfully, we have the power of God to help us in our adventure. We can speak the Good News of Christ in the power of the Holy Spirit, so that Jesus is revealed in our own time, and in our own place. *The main thing is to keep the main thing the main thing*: to know Christ, and to make Christ known.

My friend, Dr Leighton Ford, wrote these moving words, with which I would like to draw this course on evangelism to a close:

> Jesus was born in a borrowed manger. He preached from a
> borrowed boat. He entered Jerusalem on a borrowed donkey.
> He ate the Last Supper in a borrowed upper room and he was
> buried in a borrowed tomb. Now he asks to borrow the lives of
> his followers to reach the rest of the world. If we do not speak,
> then he is dumb and silent.

To conclude this course and to commission you out, I would like you to read this prayer together. And after you have done so, if you are in a group, divide into three smaller groups and pray for the Holy Spirit to fill you up and send you out in power. (If you are on your own, spend some time by yourself in prayer, asking God to do likewise.)

The main thing is to keep the main thing the main thing.

A Prayer

by J.H. Jowett

Grant that we may walk as Christ walked.
Grant that what the Spirit was in him,
    such he may be also in us.
Grant that our lives may be re-fashioned
    after the pattern of his life.
Grant that we may do today here on earth,
    what Christ would have done,
And in the way he would have done it.
Grant that we may become vessels of his grace,
instruments of his will –
To thy honour and glory.
Through Jesus Christ our Lord. Amen.

POSTSCRIPT

This has been a journey for us all: we have learned, I hope, that we are all called to the work of evangelism, that we are all called to spread the Breaking News of Christ, and that we all do so only in the power of the Spirit of God. We are not alone. God has walked the path before us, and has sent his Spirit to indwell us and empower us that for the sake of the King and the kingdom, we may truly know Christ and make Christ known.

APPENDIX I

BIBLE REFERENCES FROM SESSION I

Creation
Genesis 1:1–4; John 1:1–3; Acts 17:24–26; Colossians 1:15–16

Chaos
Genesis 3:22–24; Isaiah 53:5–6; Romans 3:23; Romans 5:12

Covenant
Genesis 9:8–11; Genesis 15:18–21:1; Exodus 19:3–6;
Jeremiah 31:31–34

Christ (the Mediator)
Mark 14:22–25; 2 Corinthians 5:18–19; Ephesians 2:14–18;
Colossians 1:19–20; 1 Timothy 2:5–6; Hebrews 9:13–15; 1 Peter 3:18

Conqueror
Luke 24:1–8; 1 Corinthians 15:21–28; 1 Corinthians 15:54–57

Certainty
Matthew 24:13–14; Romans 8:15–17; Galatians 4:6–7;
Ephesians 1:13–14; 1 John 2:3–6

Completion
Matthew 25:31–32; Revelation 21:1–2

APPENDIX 2

ORGANISATIONS QUOTED

Compassion UK
43 High Street
Weybridge
Surrey
KT13 8BB

Tel: 01932 836490
Fax: 01932 831275
E-mail: info@compassionuk.org

BIBLIOGRAPHY

John, J., *Easter Sonrise,*
Rickmansworth, Philo Trust, 2005

John, J., *More Than a Christmas Carol?*
Rickmansworth, Philo Trust, 2004

John, J. & Walley, C., *The Life: A Portrait of Jesus,*
Milton Keynes, Authentic Media, 2003

Stibbe, M., *Prophetic Evangelism,*
Milton Keynes, Authentic Media, 2004

McAlpine, Thomas H., *Facing the Powers: What are the Options?*
Oregon, Wipf & Stock, 2003

For a fuller list of resources by J.John to use in your evangelism: www.philotrust.com

The Life
A Portrait of Jesus

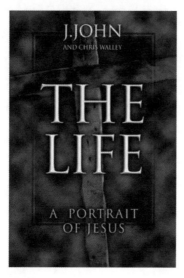

There is no denying the importance of Jesus Christ in the history of humankind.

He has walked through the last two thousand years of history, of empires, governments, political systems and philosophies and has remained as a dominant, challenging, yet mysterious presence.

In *The Life: A Portrait of Jesus* J. John and Chris Walley achieve an uncommon blend – a serious book for popular use and a popular book for serious reading.

If you want to know who Jesus is, then read *The Life* and be rewarded.